ERIN PIZZEY
COLLECTS . . .

Erin Pizzey founded the first refuge for battered wives in 1971. As a result of that work there is now refuge all over the world. She is also a writer and journalist, and a major contributor to *Cosmopolitan* magazine for several years. She has two children and two grandchildren from her first marriage. In 1980 she married Jeff Shapiro, and they now live in Santa Fe, New Mexico.

ERIN PIZZEY
Collects...

An anthology of her writing,
personally introduced

Hamlyn Paperbacks

ERIN PIZZEY COLLECTS . . .
ISBN 0 600 20686 6

First published in this collected edition
by Hamlyn Paperbacks 1983
Copyright © 1983 by Erin Pizzey

Hamlyn Paperbacks are published by
The Hamlyn Publishing Group Ltd,
Astronaut House,
Feltham, Middlesex, England

Printed and bound in Great Britain by
Cox & Wyman Limited, Reading

For DEIRDRE McSHARRY,
and for all women everywhere who
struggle through and sometimes fail.
Also for all men who truly like women
and honestly want to share our lives
with us.

CONTENTS

INTRODUCTION

As a child I was frequently punished for my inability to spell. I was described as 'lazy', 'difficult', 'sloppy'. My teachers usually ran out of adjectives, and I was then put in detention or sat outside the classroom door. Writing anything down was such an effort for me, because not only could I not spell, but also my handwriting was diabolical. I used to dread the return of stories and essays demanded by English teachers, for they were inevitably covered in red ink and rude remarks. This was made worse by the fact that my twin sister Kate could spell anything, and had beautiful handwriting.

I do, however, have one happy memory of a 'tempory teacher' who came to teach for two months. She was Maltese, and even though it is twenty-eight years or so since she taught me, I can see her vividly today. She had asked me to write two paragraphs about what *we* felt about teachers. My pen took off by itself as years of hatred flowed through the nib. I thought of all those women who had systematically destroyed me for my lack of ability and described me as 'illiterate and stupid'. I wrote my two paragraphs, or rather they wrote themselves and I followed along behind. I remember a feeling of elation as I handed in the piece of paper. It carried a clean discharge of some energy from some part of myself I didn't even know about.

The next day the teacher said she would read out the best three essays. She had warm brown eyes and a pair of round gold-rimmed, glasses. She was bubbling with laughter and, to loud giggles from the class, she read out my two paragraphs first. I can't remember what I said, but I remember a warm glow of happiness enveloping me. Somebody actually liked something I'd done. 'You can really write,' she said to me, and while she was at the school she ignored my bad handwriting and my awful spelling, and encouraged me. Poor woman – she got reams of my writing as a result. But when she left, I was back to square one. The English teacher resumed her war with me, my spelling and my handwriting.

From a tiny child, I have always been an avid reader. I'm the sort of person who can't go to the lavatory without a book in my hand. In fact, my fear of being without something new to read is akin to that of a smoker without his fags or an alcoholic without his bottle. If I go away for a few days, I take at least half a dozen books. Holidays abroad become a nightmare because I read so fast, and even if we take a suitcase of books, I am to be found skulking around bookstalls in the nearest town searching for books in English.

When I moved to Cornwall in 1964, what saved my sanity was the local mobile lending library that came round once a fortnight. You could borrow as many books as you liked, so I was in heaven. There I had plenty of time on my hands, and I began to write in the evenings when my first husband (who was a lieutenant in the Navy) was on late duty. Looking at a poem I wrote at that time: I am amazed at how prophetic it was, both about my divorce and also about my work with battered wives.

Such awful people with their simple vicious charm.
Indiscriminate coupling the coalman and the girl next door,

babies left for others to collect,
the welfare always busy with wife-beating, incest and foetid
    old age.
They all scrabble for a living in this small village,
Which has a beauty in the sun and is petrified in winter.

Everything crumbles in my house,
always smelling of damp and faulty drains,
built to exclude the sun and owned by a sterile old bitch.

Cleo survives because she's two and a half,
all the smallness seems big and exciting,
Life revolves round sweeties and us.

But we don't view each other with favour,
everything dull and covered in dust.

The sea occasionally rouses itself;
usually it is my left hand as we play a duet,
endless scales and arpeggios of boredom.

On the lighter side of things, I began to write a novel – or, like most people, a thinly disguised autobiography. I called it *One Plus One* for some reason or another. It was a comedy, and was never published. It is known affectionately by my children as 'Mummy's dirty book'. I did have an offer from a publisher who said he would publish it if I wrote another 20,000 words, but I knew I could not sustain the pace for that long, so I said no and forgot about it. When I came to write my auto-biography *Infernal Child*, I reread that first novel and was amazed at how perceptive I had been all those years ago. It was as though all the pain and anguish, and also the moments of happiness and laughter, had kept leaking out of my pen. It wasn't until we moved to London in 1965 that I had anything published. My brother arrived to stay from Rhodesia. His exuberance in our tiny flat so irritated me that I sat down and wrote about it. Because it was a funny piece, I sent it to *Punch*. To my absolute amazement they accepted it. However, I learned my first lesson about editors – they can never leave well enough alone. One wrote back offering fifteen guineas, and said I should introduce a girlfriend for the ending. I flatly refused, so Jack (my first husband), fearing the possibility of losing much needed money, wrote the ending himself. I begin my collection with that piece, because it is interesting to see how one develops and changes style as the years go by.

After that major event in my literary life, there was a resounding silence. In 1974 Penguin published *Scream Quietly, or the Neighbours Will Hear*. This was a book about my work with battered wives. Before Penguin took it, the book was turned down by most major publishers, even though battered wives had been a burning national social issue, since my Refuge – the first to open in the world – was featured in all the newspapers and on television. Most of the rejection slips stated that there was 'not sufficient interest in the subject'.

Barrie & Jenkins even suggested that I approach a television company, because they felt it might make a television series! I learned two things from this book. One: to the publishers, there was no such thing as a bad publisher, only difficult authors. Publishing used to be run by gifted amateurs, but now was only run by amateurs. The answer I discovered for myself, after dreadfully painful betrayals in the publishing world, was to find a publisher who liked books but was too gentlemanly to discuss business directly with me. This way there can be no distrust, and if a problem arises it can be resolved immediately. It never crossed my mind until I published *Prone to Violence* that it is possible to speak directly to the man who makes the final decision about your book. This is because in bad publishing houses there are layers of parasitic people who need to take raw talent and claim it as their own. They make it their business to own your work, and you will often find editors talking about 'my book'. I think the women are worse than the men, because they treat manuscripts as they would new-born babies, and become so possessive that the poor author has to fight for every original word if they get into the hands of one of these harpies.

What really made me try and be analytical about publishing in this country was the fact that my brother Danny had written a first novel set in Rhodesia. It was called *Whispering Death*. He would breeze into London with stories of huge advances and be wined and dined royally by his publisher's managing director. He was nationally known with a book already published, which sold all over the world, while my autobiography *Infernal Child* was being turned down by everybody. 'Not a Collins book,' said Collins. It wasn't anybody's book. But finally Gollancz kindly took it – and it had embarrassingly good reviews. Danny's second book was made into a film called *The Wild Geese*. Now he can command a £30,000 advance from English publishers, while I got a £4,000 advance for *The Slut's Cook Book*, which is the same as I got for *Infernal Child*, only this time I received only £1,000 on signing the contract, one thousand on handing in the manuscript, one thousand six months later, and the last thousand on publication. This meant that Jeff (my new husband) and I spent many hours agonising over our non-existent finances.

Until all writers are prepared to share their experiences with each other in an honest and open way, there is little hope of any change in relationships between authors and publishers. For far too long authors have played the game of untouchable creative geniuses who cannot sully their beautiful minds with such things as money, or contracts, or foreign rights. I have been guilty of that attitude, not because I felt I was a creative genius, but because I have been brought up to believe, like a lot of women, that I was no good at business. Just because you can't add up, you don't have to be brainwashed into believing that you are so feeble-minded that you have to allow other people to run your life for you. Actually, if you get ripped off in the world of writing, you have only yourself to blame. Anyone with a little sense, and most writers lack sense and confidence *because you tend to write in isolation*, can find out about their rights, and just what a contract should contain, by joining the Society of Authors, 84 Drayton Gardens, London SW10. There they will give you professional advice, and take up any complaint you may have.

I always believe that your Fairy Godmother eventually turns up when you most need her. In my case it was Deirdre McSharry, who is the editor of *Cosmopolitan*. She saw my letter to the *Guardian* (see page 25) and she liked it so much she wrote to me and asked me to write an article about it. From then onwards she encouraged me to write for *Cosmopolitan*. Most of these articles have been published by her. Many of them are in their original form before they were edited for the magazine. She was really the only person who ever actually said I could write. It took me years to believe her. It wasn't till I met Jeff, who confirmed what she said, that I really began to break away from many of the people surrounding me who confirmed my lack of faith in myself. In this collection I have included the odd poem where I feel it illustrates what I was feeling and doing at the time. It has been a great pleasure and a luxury for me to get this collection together, because I love writing for Deirdre, and also, because I have such a warm and loving *Cosmopolitan* readership who have stayed with me and laughed and suffered alongside me. So this book is also for them.

KARATE FOR BEGINNERS

It is a funny feeling to hold something in your hand and realise that *you* wrote it. I can see why men try so hard to write, paint, and compose music. It is probably the nearest they can get to giving birth and holding a baby. There was much of that moment of birth when I held in my hands the magazine containing my first article. I kept having to reopen it to check that it was really my name on the piece, and it wasn't going to slide off the page and hurtle into oblivion. I always resented the last paragraph of that piece, but I do have to admit I hate being edited. I don't mean the necessary correcting of grammar and punctuation, but when editors – particularly if they are over-educated and consider themselves intellectuals – can't bear to leave a rough, affectionate dialogue between an author and the reader. They flatten and fuss over the composition of a sentence until, if you are not careful, the whole piece reflects your ideas but their literary style. The answer to an editor who wants to make his – but usually *her* reputation at your expense is a straight '*No*'. If that doesn't work, get rid of her by writing to the managing director. Don't do what I have done in the past, which is to feel so grateful that anyone would publish anything I wrote, that I let myself be bullied, believe it or not, by a succession of women editors, simply because I had no confidence in my ability to write. Betraying your own writing is like allowing someone else to hurt your child while you watch. It is an agonising experience. Once I decided to stop being so feeble, I found that managing directors are more than willing to ensure that they have happy authors. Unfortunately I no longer have my original last paragraph, but here is the piece about my brother written largely by me and finished by my first husband.

He came through the door like a rogue elephant. Clutching me in his arms he said in a voice tinged with pride, 'I've been learning Karate.' After his absence for two years in Rhodesia I found my brother's presence in my small flat a little over-whelming, but I was delighted to learn that he had been putting the time to good use.

A little later my husband returned from the office in his usual state of traffic frustration and his mood was not improved when, after shaking Danny's hand, he found him-self gazing at the ceiling. 'That's only Judo,' Danny told me proudly. Muttering, my husband picked himself up off the floor. We settled down to hear tales of the African bush, crocodile fights and riots bravely quelled. Every so often I glanced at my husband, who was thoughtfully rubbing his back.

We put the mighty warrior to bed on the sofa with his feet hanging out over the edge. My sister Rosaleen arrived back from a late-night party and, in a frivolous mood brought on by gin, tickled his bare foot. The effect was instantaneous. Danny rose from the bed shouting 'YARROO' – no doubt his going-into-battle cry. There was a horrifying crunch as my sister sailed to the far end of the room and landed in a heap. She took it magnificently, and retired in silence to her bedroom. 'That was Karate,' Danny informed us both as we stood shivering in the doorway. 'You must never wake a sleeping man; it could have been anything, a deadly snake even.' He rolled over and went to sleep.

Several times during the weeks that followed he found himself unable to control his reflexes, so powerful had they become.

'We could feed him less,' said my husband with one eye on the housekeeping bills.

'Don't be silly,' I said. 'A growing boy needs his food.'

'I suppose so,' said my husband, neatly dodging Danny's outstretched hand and escaping to the kitchen to wash up. I helped, while Danny looked on scornfully, extolling the virtues of life in Rhodesia. 'We all have servants out there,' he purred. 'No housework, no washing up. Marvellous life for a woman – you'd look ten years younger if you lived that way.' My husband winced slightly and dropped a plate, but I said nothing. Danny's words had given me an idea. A girl . . . if we could just find the right one for Danny, he might lose some of his ferocity. My young sister-in-law was coming to see us next day, on her way down from university. I began to scheme.

But before she'd been in the flat half an hour she had withdrawn coldly to a corner, alienated partly by Danny's simian antics – 'A little limbering up', as he put it – and partly by his exposition of the right way to handle a woman. The main prop of his policy here seemed to be a 'sjambok' – a rhinoceros-hide whip which, he explained, would cut right to the bone at a single stroke. She left later, entirely unimpressed and muttering about 'neo-fascist brutes'.

I gathered from Danny that Karate is an old and sacred art. He only resorted to using it when death was staring him in the face, or when someone tickled his feet while he was asleep. Judo, however, was a different matter and could be playfully used on any occasion. Any guest who arrived to see us was turned upside down or swirled over his head. Bruised and exhausted, my husband sneaked in after work and retired to the bedroom before he could be jovially encouraged to try a little judo.

The flat would shudder and shake with the movement of Danny walking to and fro. 'The call of the wild,' he would murmur with a faraway look in his blue eyes. 'Can't stand this enclosed feeling.'

'How about the wide open spaces of Hyde Park?' my husband would suggest. 'There are some very good benches you could stretch out on.'

'Must learn to live with it,' Danny would gravely say. 'Can't spend my life in the bush with only my thirty askaris to depend on me.'

'What you need to depend on you is a woman,' I said, harking back to my beloved theme.

'Don't want to get lumbered with women,' he snapped. 'Too busy keeping fit.'

'You've got a point there,' I said, but I was mentally going over all the girls we knew. There had to be one somewhere who could tame him.

I waited nervously for the day when Danny, as he had warned me, would be overcome by circumstances and lay some man flat in the streets of London with one mighty Karate swipe. Day after day he would arrive with harrowing stories of the policeman who had narrowly escaped total annihilation, the parking-meter man who only just avoided death, or the shopkeeper who, on putting his hand on Danny's arm, had fallen back amazed at the rippling muscles which knotted beneath his fingers.

One morning I was just straightening out the flat after a particularly violent eruption of Danny getting up and leaving, when the doorbell rang. It was Danny back again with, wonder of wonders, an attractive girl on his arm. He ushered her in with a magnificent flourish; she gazed up at him in wide-eyed admiration. I was delighted. We talked, and Danny, glowing with pride, slipped his arms round her slight form. She moved her right hip almost imperceptibly and Danny crashed spinning to the floor. He leapt up and rushed at her with a shout of joy. They writhed and struggled and then suddenly she was on her back with him kneeling on her shoulders – they both looked ecstatic. 'Isn't she marvellous,' he beamed up at me. 'Her father runs a judo club. Here, let me help you put those vases straight.'

(Originally published in *Punch*, January 1966)

WAITING WOMEN

'Waiting Women' was written at the request of the editor of the *Sunday Telegraph*'s opinion piece. I was so amazed that he should ask me to write for so august a journal that I wrote the first draft of this article immediately and sent it to him by return of post. He was a kindly, long-suffering man. He wrote back saying that my article had many good ideas, but he had never seen an eleven-line sentence. That has always been a problem for me and for Bernard Levin. Except that Bernard's sentences are a carefully constructed work of art, and mine are a result of my rambling Irish brain that only produces a full-stop when it runs out of steam. I sat down again and rewrote it more carefully. From preparing this article I learned to write simple, short sentences. Every time I started to take off like a steam train, I'd have to haul myself back. 'Cut out the crap,' I often say to myself when I find I'm making a simple statement in a confused or pretentious way. This article was, and still is, a deeply held view that our society ignores women and their potential as community workers and nurturers at our peril.

'The hand that rocks the cradle rules the world' was once a comforting maxim. Generations of women knew perfectly well that they were the corner-stones and architects of their own small communities and that the overall responsibility for the welfare of the village-pump life lay in the hands of the women who surrounded it. Today the pump is replaced by a launderette, and the women who live round it peer down from their highrise flats. Behind those front doors lies a reservoir of volunteers who would benefit the community and themselves

if they had the opportunity. The 'Good Neighbours' scheme launched some time ago by Mr Ennals [then Secretary of State for Social Services] needs all the encouragement it can get; but it could also be amended to save money, by doing away with many paid 'Welfare' workers.

Before the Industrial Revolution women of each community were the midwives, health visitors, social workers, probation officers, marriage guidance counsellors, citizens' advice officer, samaritans – all at no cost to the country in financial terms – and their work was tremendously rewarding emotionally. Men and women created the necessities of life within their own homes. Then the Industrial Revolution destroyed their home-grown industries and sent them out to supervise the machines which replaced them. Having lost the personal satisfaction of creating a length of cloth or a cabinet, people sought to placate their sense of loss and desolation with financial rewards. The women found they had taken jobs in the new factories in order to be able to afford the goods they once created in their own homes. The only real advantage was that they were able, too, to earn something which helped alleviate the often crippling poverty.

Unfortunately, with the traditional 'people who cared for others' in society deserting their communities, there was nobody left to help give birth, feed the sick, tend the dying and care for the old. So a whole new profession was born: the professional 'carers' or social workers. They were not part of the communities they served, and they had to be 'trained'. But loving and caring are both qualities taught by generations of mothers to their own children. Traditionally mothers trained their small daughters who followed round after them, learning to deliver babies, cook for the hungry and care for the elderly. Those early days were not a haze of golden pleasure, and there is no doubt that modern medicine has made an enormous improvement to the physical welfare of the nation, but in caring for our physical selves in terms of better housing, health and education, we have forgotten our spiritual selves. We have not found the real substitute for the ordinary people who cared for one another.

Puzzled administrators of the new profession had to devise techniques to replace years of maturing experience. Books were hastily written and a special language was devised to make sure that no one except the initiated could lay claim to the title of 'social worker'. Sadly, when the women of the country turned round, they found they had been usurped. Middle-class women who had always worked within their villages were now sneered at as 'do-gooders'. They were told that the local village drunk had an 'unresolved hostility conflict that could only be cured through more eye-to-eye contact and the building up of a one-to-one relationship with his social worker'. Timidly the do-gooder might point out that the drunk had had one-to-one relationships with most of the women in the village and lots of eye-to-eye contact with the local magistrate, and that a sharp clip round the earhole from the local bobby usually did the trick for at least six months. But the professional social workers only had to wave a bit of paper which said that he or she had read several hundred books, attended thousands of lectures, and so on to prove they knew best.

Working-class women who were the backbone of the country were told by 23-year-old college graduates that they were meddling. They too faded away.

The army of professional carers still grows at vast cost to the country, feeding like leeches on the misery of the poor and needy. The tentacles lead back to the Department of Health and Social Security, which squats at the Elephant and Castle in London and, like the elephant, gives laborious birth to reams of paper, and stamps heavily on any effort at voluntary participation.

But there is a silent army of people much more able to care efficiently sitting waiting to be called. There are huge organisations like the Women's Institutes, Townswomen's Guilds, Mothers' Unions, Ladies' Circles – women whose children have grown up and gone, widows, pensioners, millions of women with time on their hands and a wealth of untapped experience. I remember watching a social worker spend days delivering bulbs donated by a well-meaning businessman for distribution to the blind. I have watched social workers spend hours doing jobs a voluntary worker attached to a local office could have done easily. Above all, a voluntary worker could spend valuable hours talking to the lonely and the old, who call into social services offices just to chat.

There are thousands of 60-year-old women cleaning floors, or working in part-time jobs to supplement Social Security benefits. We are wasting their experience and information.

I wonder which government will have the good sense to prune down the huge social services departments and give the country back to its waiting women?

(Originally published in *Sunday Telegraph*, 17 April 1977)

LITTLE BOY BLUES

This is the letter that literally changed my life: in 1977 Barbara Cartland wrote, and had published, a letter to the *Guardian*, stating that men should literally sweep women off their feet and carry them swooning across saddles in their powerful, muscular arms to their tents in the desert of Wandsworth, or something like that. I had just recently separated from my first husband, and after seventeen years of marriage was finding it very difficult to make relationships with other men. For many women of my age the breakdown of a marriage really throws you out into a world where you almost have to begin all over again. You feel so silly even inviting a man to dinner for the first time. My first dinner was a disaster, because no sooner had the poor man seated himself at the table than my son took an instant dislike to him and kept charging into the room shouting 'adulterer' at the poor fellow. Needless to say I never saw him again.

It is all very well for us to be told that all we want and need are marvellous, tender, loving, adult, mature men, but what we aren't told is where to find them. I know plenty of adult women, but I can count on the fingers of my left foot the number of grown-up males I have ever met.

I came across a woman the other day and I asked her if she had ever met a man as opposed to an enlarged six-year-old. To my surprise she said she had, but added that he had died. I'm not surprised. It must have been like being a dodo or the Loch Ness monster, and he may well have got killed in the rush to his door. Why is it that girls grow into women, but boys grow into large Peter Pans?

I have come to the sad conclusion, having passed through the usual stages of rage, grief and depression, that it is not a question of men oppressing women but mothers infantalising their sons and then handing the damaged wrecks on to their daughters-in-law, with advice on how to wash, clean and cook for them in the style they have always been accustomed to. Far too many women marry for a meal ticket, hate the whole business, resent their husbands, and then turn to their sons, whom they seduce in such a way that the boy is enmeshed in a net that holds him captive. A child is not supposed to hate his mother, who gave up her life/health/job/food/varicose veins to make him a beautiful little Lord Fauntleroy. But he can hate all other women and spend the rest of his life kicking their teeth in – using also indiscriminate charm, promises and baby talk, all of which worked so well on Mummy.

In between times he can be seen gazing into mirrors sniffing a pale white narcissus. No one can love him like his mother, so he's always looking. He thinks he's a fabulous lover. So does any woman who sleeps with him, until she realises that she is just something that comes between him and his press-ups. I think we face a crisis at this point in time that affects all women – a plague of 'smothered' men – and we have to look very carefully at how we are bringing up our sons.

I believe that men and women are two entirely different species, so blurring the sex roles produces a strange mutant with a foot in both camps. I was running round the house the other day with a can of air-freshener, and I was about to squirt it in my son's room when he stopped me.

'This room smells,' I said . . . 'It smells of sweat, fags and beer, and that's how I like to smell,' he said – point taken.

I like the house to smell of sugar and spice and all things nice . . . Maybe boys should be allowed their snails and puppydog tails, and then maybe there'll be some men around.

Yours in desperation,
Erin Pizzey
8 July 1977

THE NARCISSISTIC MAN

In the confusion of my feelings at that time, I felt very cross when I read the original *Guardian* item and very pleased when they printed my retort. A few days after it appeared I got a letter from Deirdre McSharry, who asked me if I would like to write an article for *Cosmopolitan* about 'Narcissistic Man'. It was a subject close to my heart, and this time I was much more disciplined about writing it. It struck a big chord in many women readers, who wrote to me and told me about their lives.

There are no men more lovable or attractive than the true narcissus; because he loves only himself he takes the greatest care of his person, and he develops all his useful sociable abilities so he is charm personified. His stock-in-trade is the vulnerable lost-little-boy looking for someone just like you to care for him. Once he is resident he turns into a petulant six-year-old. These are the men who have been ruined by their mothers. However, it is not the mothers who suffer the damage but his relationships with all other women who fling themselves hopelessly into his arms, then lie bruised and bleeding from his rejection, muttering, 'Where did I go wrong?' My advice to anyone contemplating a relationship with a true narcissus is – Don't . . . not unless you are absolutely aware of what you are doing, or unless you are a masochist. You can expect no more from him than a few fleeting moments of intense happiness, which he will offer you when he flutters past on one of his many missions of tending all his interests.

Behind every narcissus there crouches a spider of a mother. Surprisingly, she is rarely a dragon of a figure. Mostly she looks like an Oxo advert mum. Warm as an apple dumpling.

She loves her son and will do anything for him. In fact she always does everything for him. She cleans, cooks, washes, irons and makes his bed. He need not have been born with limbs at all. All this she does with a smile on her lips and a hand covering her breast or clapped to her brow, because she is always in pain but it has never stopped her caring for her own little boy.

The reason she adopts this attitude to her son is because she is actually bored and disillusioned with her husband. She is usually a woman who has opted to marry rather than achieve any of her other potentials. Once the wedding, the presents and the three-piece suite wear off, she takes a good long look at her husband and discovers the awful truth: unlike the fairy story where the princess kisses the frog and he becomes a prince, in life if you kiss a frog he just becomes a self-satisfied frog. In the picture-books the prince goes clip-clop round the countryside slaying dragons, but her husband just picks his nose and watches the telly. For a high-minded woman who gave up her all to marry this man, it is all too much, and she feels extremely disillusioned. So, when her son comes along, she very soon decides to give herself completely to this tiny, helpless, little male and fashion her own version of a knight in shining armour. From then on she disregards her husband, who is pushed into the background, so he soon gives up trying at all and just sits quietly in his chair, dreaming of the office typist.

These mothers love their sons best when they are clean and tidy, because dirt – next to sex – is one of the seven deadly sins. There are family snapshots of the little boy in a lacy white dress at an age when other little boys are romping in the mud. Of course, he cannot play with those sort of children, because they are not good enough for him. Because the mother has emotionally rejected the father, she clings to her son in a way that is highly sexual, though she rarely realises it and would retire to bed with a migraine if it were mentioned to her. Sex is disgusting and she has been known to put brown paper under her son's sheets to see that he does not abuse himself, and thus ruin his perfect eyesight. As he gets older and becomes interested in girls, she becomes more demanding.

Her ambition is for her son to become Prime Minister, and

towards that end she is prepared to bully, cajole, tutor, lie, cheat and nag him until his days are spent desperately trying to achieve her ambitions. As we have only one Prime Minister at a time in this country, England is full of generals, admirals, heads of corporations, MPs, and suchlike, who will always feel they have failed their mother – such is her power. She realises that in between the solid grind he must have a girlfriend, but, again, only the best will do. And her idea of the most suitable girl is a member of the royal family, or a friend's daughter with spots and a cast-iron vagina.

There is very little likelihood of any early sexual encounters for the boy, because the mother has a habit of bursting through the door in the house offering food and tea, or staying awake until all hours of the early morning stirring a saucepan of Horlicks for his goodnight drink. She likes it best when he is ill. He soon likes to be ill, because it results in an orgy of caring: a procession of food, books, cool-hands-on-fevered-brow type treatment. Who else will care for him like his Mummy cares for him? Who else, indeed? Even if he hates her at times – can't stand the interference, the moaning, the clinging – how can you hate anyone who is so good to you? If he's nasty she cries and bakes his favourite cake. He feels guilty – he always feels guilty, and for many adolescent years he struggles with hate, guilt and love. Some men break away and see the relationship for what it truly is. Many do not.

Sons of those types of mothers are usually chained to them for life. Their relationships with other women are transitory, and their central relationship is always with the devouring mother. They are at their most dangerous when they marry. Too many women mistake the hurt wandering little boy for a potential husband. The problem is that, like Peter Pan, they never grow up. They expect the same caring from their wives as they had from their mothers. They make their homes and their wives a 'safe place' for their forays into the outside world. In their heart-of-hearts they tell themselves they love their wives but they roam from affair to affair. And every time the new mistress starts to make any demands on him he kicks her teeth in and returns home. The truth is that there are iron bars around his soul. He loves no one but himself, and having been so over-possessed by his mother, he will never allow himself to be trapped again. His mother taught him nothing of love and compassion; rather she taught him all the material things of life, and these he trusts. He dresses well, eats well, is charming, and when he looks deep into his beloved's eyes he is usually checking his hair-style.

You can tell the wife of a narcissus – she usually looks plain and dowdy, because he hogs the bathroom and spends most of the time in front of the mirror. Furthermore she has a peculiar goosestep which she develops from stepping over his prostrate body while he does his exercises all over the house. Sometimes a wife will accept him for what he is. She knows that she will only know a few of his friends because a narcissus keeps all his relationships in different compartments. He will always be late for everything, because then he can make an entrance. He will be generous with money when it directly benefits himself, otherwise he is extremely mean and rather expects to be supported. He can talk for hours about himself but little else interests him. He will probably expect his wife to be very meticulous around the house, because he has internalised Mummy's standards. He is not a good long-term lover because, while he is unusually athletic, he cannot give of himself. As a result, in the short term he is a good stud, in the long term the woman feels herself bereft.

The woman who decided to accept such a man for what he is, usually treats him like one of the children of the family, and sometimes that can work. However, the saddest women are those who believe his stories of his unhappy married life. What they don't realise is that he is the eternal wooer. It is the chase that excites him. His vision of himself as the romantic lover. The hours of choosing the clothes, the bathing, the after-shave, the dinner for two at an expensive restaurant (on expenses of course), the intrigue, the passion; and when it is spent, which is as soon as the woman expects anything from him, it is finished – he's gone. She joins the queue of women who wait by the phone, who cry into their pillows, wondering where they went wrong. They didn't go wrong; they just didn't realise that a narcissus is a flower that always leans elegantly away from its fellow flowers. The only relationships he can make will be port-of-call relationships – like a ship in the night.

If you marry one, stay if you can accept the loneliness; if not, get out and find a man who can give of himself – there are a few around. If you are thinking of having an affair with one, visit his mother. Remember the story of the wicked princess who said to the son of the queen, 'Bring me your mother's heart and I will be thine.' Sadly, he killed his mother and tore out her heart. He rushed back to his princess and on the way he tripped. The heart rolled down the hill, and as he bent to pick it up it whispered 'Son, did thee hurt thyself?' . . . If she's like that mother, give up. And if you have sons, try to love them wisely and not too well.

(Originally published March 1978, reprinted by kind permission of *Cosmopolitan* magazine)

BATTERED MEN

Way back in 1978 I was trying to get people to heed me when I pointed out that battering was not only done by men. Nobody wanted to listen. Women preferred to think of themselves as always the victims, and men who are terrified of violent women are all too ready to agree with this in public – but in the privacy of their homes and clubs commiserate with each other. On a lecture tour of American refuges I was upbraided again and again by the extreme members of the Women's Movement for daring to say that a woman could be responsible for the violence in a relationship. I never understood why it has to be an *either or* situation. In my considerable experience, both men and women can be violent. The answer is to *understand* the problem, not to deny it.

We have heard the case against the wife-batterer time and time again, but very rarely can I get people to hear me when I point out that there are just as many violent women in our society as men. This is partly because we like to maintain the 'madonna' image of womanhood, and nice women just aren't supposed to be violent. I think the other reason is because women tend to express their violence in a much more subtle manner; but it is no less terrifying for their victims, and no less damaging to themselves.

If you accept that the family is the primary socialising agency in a child's life, then it follows that for the first few years the child will use the parents as its model. The boys of the family will adopt the father's patterns as their own, and the girls will imitate their mother's behaviour. By the time the child is three it will have internalised much of the parents' behaviour, and their reality will belong to the child. How the parents relate to each other, to their children, and then the outside world will be transmitted to the children, who in turn will adopt their parents' attitudes, and the pattern is thus set firm for the rest of their lives. It is not generally realised that those first few years in a child's life are vital, and any damage done at that time can mean a lifelong sentence of misery for the child – and for everyone else who crosses its path.

Aggression is a natural part of human nature: like hunger and fear, aggression is useful because it is a survival instinct. And so the small baby uses it to call attention to discomfort and pain. Around eighteen months the baby realises the power that aggression gives and starts to throw temper tantrums. In a normal family these tantrums are dealt with quite firmly and kindly, because it is not considered acceptable behaviour. But in a violent family that baby will see that grown-ups throw temper tantrums and consider it an acceptable and a legitimate way of getting exactly what they want. Then not only does the child mimic the adult, but also learns the rewards of violence. While the normal family is busily teaching its baby that he or she must develop a frustration level and wait to achieve what it wants, the violent family is teaching the child exactly the opposite – that violent behaviour will achieve what you want *immediately*.

Now it seems to me, from the many thousands of families I have dealt with, that where the mother is violent the girls are likely to be violent. Either they imitate her and act violently themselves, or they become violence-prone and seek out violent relationships. Where the father is violent and the mother passive and withdrawn, the boys will be violent and the girls will usually take the mother's role and be cowed. Either way, the damage is life-scarring.

The above description is a simple explanation of a very complicated human condition. There is one other situation that will create a violent woman, and this is what I call the 'princess' syndrome. Here, in a family which may not be violent at all, a deal has been done between the daughter and the father which excludes the mother (sometimes the mother colludes and bows out gracefully) and the daughter takes the place of the wife in her father's affections. In an ordinary family this may mean that she is spoilt rotten by Dad, whereas in a violent family, in which the father sexually assaults her, the daughter becomes a willing partner. Either way the girl reigns at home, and her every whim is indulged by her adoring father. Her tantrums are considered simply as high spirits, and it doesn't take her very long to discover that her power over her father gives her access to money and all it can buy.

Because most mothers find this relationship very puzzling and are hurt and jealous, they withdraw from their daughters or have screaming rows with them. Here father comforts the daughter, who can soon out-scream and out-rage anybody who tries to take her on. This early spoiling means that the girl develops no frustration level. Like the girl from the violent home, she also learns that violence gets her what she wants immediately, and her pattern is set for a disastrous relationship. There are many princesses around, and because they have been used to seducing Daddy either emotionally or physically from a very early age, they are past masters at manipulation. They will never love anybody else but Daddy; however, as they turn their beady little eyes outwards they see the endless possibilities of ever increasing material gain in the pockets of other men.

A violent woman can be great fun to be with. Just as many women are attracted to violent men because the Peter Pan element in their personality is very appealing, so a violent woman usually has a lifestyle that is charged with energy, excitement and drama. Wherever she is, things just start to happen, and provided she is in a good mood it's party time. But when she gets angry – and that can be in a flash – it's seconds out, and someone gets hurt – very rarely her. The moment the tantrum is over, her hurt child comes out and no one can be more appealingly or genuinely sorry. This is why many men don't leave women who behave in the most atrocious fashion. But pity and compassion make poor bed-fellows, and women who don't come to terms with their violence grow old disgracefully, usually destroying their partners and their children.

There is also an erotic element in a violent woman; she gives an aura of power and control that many men find a challenge. Often a man will believe that he can overpower and control her, and this rouses his hunting instinct. When this kind of relationship arises, it is very hard for either side to let go. It usually occurs when two violent people decide to take each other on: they push each other to the limit and over it, crushing anyone in the way. It seems to the outside world like the most disastrous relationship ever, but they are actually satisfying mutual needs.

I saw a woman the other day who was so badly beaten her face was hardly recognisable. She peered at me through puffed eyelids and it was hard to hear her through her swollen lips. But she was telling me about Ian, her man, with whom she had lived for fifteen years. He had just beaten her up again . . . She had come to me to tell me in case she should die, but she had no intention of leaving him. She talked of him with such love and warmth that I knew they would stay together, even as she lifted her chin to show me a huge thick scar where he had tried to slash her neck. Then she pulled back her jumper and showed me ridges of scarring where she had tried to kill herself.

Both of them were terribly violent. They were in their forties. Ian's parents were farmers. His mother died giving birth to him, for which he never forgave himself. His father was a cruel bully, and Ian remembered being taken to hospital by his sister after a particularly bad beating that broke both his legs. She had to carry him on her back across the fields. Many nights he was thrown out of the house by his father and slept in the barns, cold and hungry. She cried while she talked about his childhood, and I cried when I heard about hers. Raped by her father, beaten and starved by her mother, she remembered lying in bed with her mother while strange men came into the room, had sex with her mother and then left ten shillings on the table. She had been in every girls' reform school, and then prison, for fighting, stealing and fraud.

Even though their relationship seemed awful to outsiders, she said that the only other human being in the world who could love her, damaged as she was, was him. He felt the same about her.

It is one thing when two equally-matched violent people get into a relationship, but quite another when a man from a normal loving childhood decided to live with a violent woman. I have had men come to see me because they have been branded wife-batterers by onlookers. They admit they have hit their partners, but they swear they are not violent – just pushed beyond their limit. It doesn't take long for me to work out if this is true or not.

Mr M came to see me, and as he explained his own self-disgust and despair, he began to cry. He had been married for ten years, although the relationship had always been tempestuous. He married Jane because she was an orphan in the storm. He believed that marriage and lots of love would settle her down and cure her insecurity. She, once safe from the storm, decided that she would have everything she wanted. She spent money like water; if she didn't get money, he got no sex. If he had no money left, she opened accounts. He had a good job, but she made promotion hard for him by getting drunk, insulting the senior men, and having a series of affairs with the younger men, about which she would boast.

They had one child, not because she wanted children, but, as she told him in a more spiteful moment, it assured her the house and half his income until the boy was sixteen. Recently she had taken to drinking a lot more and taunting him in screaming rows. Finally, after the screaming had harrowed him beyond measure, he lashed out by hitting her across the face. The episode that brought him to me was when he once found his hands around her throat, and he panicked.

It is a fairly typical story. He was an emotionally battered husband. He had to look at why he married her. Lots of other men would have seen the warning signals and kept away. He had to consider why he had stayed ten years and not left her before. I had to point out to him that far from stopping her, any act of violence on his part would only feed her need for drama and excitement.

Finally, as she seemed to me to be organising to take his house, money and son, I said that if he was prepared to see me for a while on a regular basis, I would write a report for any court proceedings she would take against him. I am aware of the danger of women misusing the sanctuary of a refuge, and it must not be used as a weapon against an innocent man.

Violent women are very lonely women. They can't make good relationships so they tend to leave a trail of bodies lying in their past. They yell, scream and bully, but really they are very

36

frightened. They always play games. They manipulate everybody around them, keeping themselves safe in the middle. They gossip, spread rumours, find every chink in anyone's defences. They go round with an invisible dagger, plunging it deep into everyone's back. The more intelligent the woman, the more dangerous she is. Far too many people walk round with bleeding wounds caused by their early upbringing, looking for someone else to act as a bandage. The answer for people who blindly make disastrous relationships is to consider that you don't have to make your past your future. It takes a lot of courage to discover yourself, but it is an inner journey full of lovely surprises.

(Originally published December 1978, as 'Battered husbands', reprinted by kind permission of *Cosmopolitan* magazine)

A WOMAN, A DOG AND
A WALNUT TREE

Well, after violent women I wrote a piece about 'battered women'. These are women who are 'victims of another person's violence', as opposed to 'violence-prone women' who are victims of their own violence.

'I am an ex-"battered wife" and have finally left my husband, taking my daughter who is nine months old. She was born with a congenital dislocation of the hip. She was being treated in ——, where I come from, and the decision to interrupt her treatment was a very difficult one to make, despite my desire to leave the horrors of being married to a nightly wife-beater and alcoholic. I will not go into the details of the terrible cruelty that I have suffered, although I would be more than willing if they would be of any use to you.

'My husband is a general practitioner, and whilst at medical school was an amateur boxer, so he had plenty of brawn as well as brain, plus enough money to keep him well supplied with as much whisky as he wanted.

'I have left him four times previously but always ended up going back to him because he would find out where I was – usually with my elderly parents – and harass and threaten them at all hours of the day and night, at the same time promising to mend his ways and pleading with me to go back because he loved me.

'He is an excellent doctor and a much-respected public citizen. He was, however, on his own insistence, my own doctor and treated me with utter contempt even when I threatened to miscarry at twelve weeks of pregnancy, and also during and after my baby's delivery. (I gave birth to her at home without a midwife present.)

'This last time, having made the decision to get away and stay away, regardless of the consequences, I was fortunate in that my brother and his wife, whom I had not seen for years, suddenly stepped in and offered me accommodation in their small flat. I am a qualified teacher and now have a job, an excellent solicitor and a very understanding GP.

'I have been away now for two months, and after experiencing the immediate relief of no more mental and physical cruelty, I am now trying to adjust to a very uncertain future, accompanied by continual nightmares and depression.

'I always felt I had no one to turn to; my family lived a long way away and I was too ashamed to tell friends who all thought the world of my husband. I often thought, "If only there were someone to turn to, somewhere to go."

'I am lucky in that I have a strong personality and also have kind relatives and the knowledge of how to go about getting supplementary benefit. I have a good solicitor, who is working hard to try and get me a legal separation and custody of my child as quickly as possible.'

This is one of the many heart-rending letters that have come to me over the years that I have been running the refuge. The question one is always asked is: 'Why do women get into violent relationships with men?' In the beginning, I was told by social workers and sociologists that wife-battering was a working-class phenomenon. 'You see,' they would say, wagging their fingers at me, 'the working-class man is inarticulate. He cannot express his anger or frustration in any other way than by lashing out at his wife . . . In the North, of course, a woman who doesn't have a black eye on a weekend doesn't feel truly loved.' I used to feel like howling with rage at the smug, self-confident attitude that allowed so-called 'professionals' to ignore the pain and torture that occur daily behind the portcullis of an Englishman's castle.

Of course, society has historically done little until recent times to protect women from violence. It was perfectly legal a hundred years ago for a man to beat his wife, provided he used a stick no bigger than his thumb. This is where the old saying 'rule of thumb' comes from. In 1878, Frances Power Cobbe wrote an impassioned plea asking for the protection of women. Her paper was called 'Wife Torture in England'.* She got a member of Parliament to ask Disraeli, who was Prime Minister at the time, what could be done to offer protection. The Prime Minister was moved to tears and promised that action would be taken. He set up a select committee to look into the problem. They sat. They reported. And nothing happened.

The only time women and children take precedence is when a ship goes down, and then it is usually too late. However, what annoyed me about that hundred year-old paper is how exact the author's findings were. She noted the awful habits of the Liverpool men who wore what they called 'kicking boots' which they used indiscriminately on their women. She talked of the terrible torture inflicted on the helpless women and children all over England, and she made a very strong point of proclaiming that it was most certainly not just the working-class men who beat their women. Family violence cut across all social barriers, and even the most noble families of the day had their fair share of bullies and tyrants.

While this was going on in England, women in America were taking up the fight. In 1824 the Mississippi Supreme Court ruled that '. . . the husband should be permitted the right to chastise his wife moderately in cases of great emergency without subjecting himself to prosecution and shame.' The American women had already been in the fore-front of the battle to free the slaves. This having been done, they were faced with their own slavery, and they took up the cudgel on behalf of their sisters. As in England, the subject slid into obscurity until it surfaced again in 1971 at the first refuge in the world to open its doors unconditionally to battered women and their children.

What people from the outside – that is, people who have no conception of what it is like to be in a violent relationship – don't understand is how a violent relationship can warp and distort even the most stable of women. I have already written about violent women, and in this article I will concentrate on

*Partly reproduced in *Prone to Violence* by Erin Pizzey and Jeff Shapiro.

women who by accident, or because they genuinely believe that love will change all, try their best to stay with and care for a man who is violent and abusive.

A second letter is the story of one such woman:

'I was married in March 1964 at the age of sixteen. My husband, an undergraduate, was twenty-five. We were very happy until after the birth of the fourth child. By this time my husband had graduated, taken a job as a lecturer, given it up, started his own contracting business and was rapidly becoming a successful businessman. At first his drinking was restricted to weekends, then it became much more frequent, until Christmas 1966, by which time he was drinking every evening after work until long after midnight.

'He would arrive home in a very drunken state and complain bitterly about everything I did or said to him. He was frightening when in this sort of aggressive mood but never made an attempt to hit me until 1969, on my son's fourth birthday. He arrived home at 9.30 p.m. and insisted I get James out of bed, in order to give him a present. After refusing, I eventually agreed to let him see James in the bedroom, but he picked him up and brought him into the kitchen, where he was very insulting to me and called me a slut and a whore. I asked for an explanation; he told me he owed me nothing. I said I was about sick of his behaviour and wanted to put James back in bed. My husband refused to hand him over. James was crying and reaching out to me. I took James from my husband. He tried to get him back but James clung to me. After about three or four minutes my husband grabbed James and punched me behind the right ear at the same time. He picked up the bread-knife and threatened to put it through my throat. I told him I had taken my fill of him – threats, insults and now assaults. I said I was leaving and taking our children. His reply was that I could get out, but if I tried to take the children he would kill me. I grabbed my coat and left the flat. I stayed the night in the convent where the children went to nursery shool, collected them the following day and went home to my parents. I stayed away for nearly three weeks, during which time my husband visited us and asked me to return. After he gave me an undertaking never to touch me again, I went home. I was back seven months before the next assault.

'During this time my husband was becoming increasingly possessive, stopping me from visiting my mother and godmother. He stopped me from communicating with all my past friends, saying that I should mix with married women. When I did this, he said my married friends were a bad influence on me – in fact every friend I have ever had was bad in his eyes. It occurs to me now that they were a threat to him; I had someone to turn to when he attacked me. Also, he may have been afraid that they would persuade me to leave him.

'On this second assault, his friend came home with him at 3 a.m. I got up when told to because I feared another beating if I didn't. We sat and discussed music and politics for about an hour, then my husband suddenly began shouting at me and calling me names. I went to bed, then I was called back. I made a bed up for the guest. My husband suddenly accused me of flirting with his friend and 'fancying' him. I told him I never noticed another man from the day I became engaged to him. He called me a liar and hit me in the mouth. My top lip was split, and my mouth badly puffed and bruised. We went to bed, and after refusing to have intercourse with my husband he hit me on the back of the head, causing my nose to spurt blood, and tried to suffocate me with the pillow. I reported this assault to the hospital, because after the first incident I discovered that GPs don't want to know about husband-and-wife disputes and it is impossible to obtain a legal separation or divorce without some sort of medical evidence. Three days later, I returned from shopping to find all my clothes, including boots and shoes, ripped or slashed. My husband told me the children had mentioned a man being in the hospital; he assumed I was having an affair with this person, who in fact was the brother of the woman who collected them from school. I had only the clothes I was wearing, and had to ask my parents for money to buy clothes before I could return to college the following Monday.

'After this he beat me regularly every four months, always after a drinking bout. Most of the blows were to my face and head, particularly my eyes; it is significant that from having perfect eyesight at sixteen, I now have great difficulty in reading the advertisements in the Tube. I tried to leave my husband. I contacted the Catholic Housing Aid Society, the Samaritans, the NSPCC, the housing department of the local authority. No one wanted to know. It was always the same. "We can't give you somewhere to live because your husband can come back on us." "Obtain a separation and then we will help you." There's one problem here. The courts will not grant separation orders if the woman doesn't get out. They say: "If the situation is intolerable as you describe, how have you managed to stick it for this length of time?" It's one vicious circle of very large perimeter, with the woman in the middle and the husband and bureaucracy hitting out from all points.

'On one occasion, after strapping my dislocated wrist, a sympathetic doctor advised me to contact the social services. This I did as soon as the doors were open on Monday morning. I was told I must give my marriage a chance. I had been married for five and a half years at the time, so I thought the advice rather irrelevant. When I told the social worker this she got quite abrupt with me and said I could not be given temporary accommodation, but they would send someone to see my husband. This was done, and after four abortive attempts the social worker finally got him at home. He was very nice to her at first, then ended up telling her to get out and mind her own business, and said he would look after the children if I left.

'The next time I contacted this department was after my doctor had already rung them and impressed upon them that it was imperative that I be taken out of this situation. They told me to leave the children with my husband. He would look after them. I pointed out that three weeks before he had been placed on probation and had another assault case coming up the following week. I was told that if they felt he wouldn't care for the children (however, they had no evidence to this effect), they would be taken into care. All the children were being affected by this disturbing atmosphere, having witnessed almost every attack on me, so I didn't think it would be wise to take the social worker's advice.

'I realised that I would have to stick it out until I found an open door to a better life. I have saved over £500 and intended to get enough for a deposit on a house, when I returned to college. My husband found out about my savings and stopped giving me any money. I went through the money and then, when it was gone, gave up college and went to work. At this time I didn't know of the existence of social security.

'Between 1969 and 1972 I had suffered twenty-seven brutal attacks, including ten which required me to be admitted to hospital for two days or more. Once I lost the baby I was expecting. The police came on all of these occasions and, while sympathetic, did nothing, except to tell me to take him to court. I was reluctant to do this, knowing he would attack me seriously, and maybe the result would be fatal. However, in the end I could stand it no more. After attempting to strangle me with our telephone wire he was charged by me and was bound over to keep the peace and fined £25. I had to pay this money out of my housekeeping money. Before this case got to court he came home drunk and tried to persuade me to drop the case. When I refused he got into a rage and beat me so much that he split my head open. He received a three-year probation period for this offence. He was given a suspended prison sentence when within a month he was in court again for grievous bodily harm. Two weeks after the latest court case my husband ripped my coat, kicked my pet terrier in the face and nearly broke my finger in an attempt to get my wedding ring, which he eventually bent and threw out of the window. The incidents took place on our eighth wedding anniversary. I left the following day. My husband tried to see me at my parents' home. He was let in twice and forced his way in another night. I was along at home with my eighteen-year-old sister and the children. The police removed him, and after he received another eight summonses he fled to Ireland. He was back in this country after one month, coming round frequently to our flat, which by this time I was occupying. After hitting me, trying to prevent me taking the children out and breaking down a door which fell onto my daughter's bed and narrowly missing her head, he moved into the flat, which I immediately left.

'People say that the reason so many women suffer this sort of treatment is that women don't know their rights. Well, I knew mine. I informed my solicitor that I wanted to apply for an injunction. He agreed to do this, but first of all tried to tell me I had to move out. I proved to him that I had nowhere to go, then my husband left. He then said I had no need for an injunction. After I left finally in November 1972 I asked my solicitor to seek an injunction again. He said the court would take the view that I had somewhere to stay and would not grant the injunction. I took his word for it and now my husband has given up our flat. I am homeless and penniless with many scars both physical and mental to remind me of life with a jealous, alcoholic husband.'

So far, I have talked about women already married and trapped. What about women and young girls who are living with someone yet still have the freedom to choose to get out? The problem is that a violent man can seem like a life-sentence. The fact that you are living with him, or even going out with him, can be enough for his jealous, paranoid behaviour to take over your life and personality. It usually starts in the classroom with the James Bond of the fifth form. The boy every girl wants to go out with. The one with the mouth and the money (usually cadged off someone else). The boy who doesn't let his girl out of his sight. (What he does out of hers is perfectly all right.) The boy who is desperate to get married, often because his own family is violent and because he believes that if he married, he would never hit his wife, or because he is on the run again from his over-protective mother in the belief that it will all be different with his own true love.

Type A, the man from the violent family, is liable to be the most physically violent. He has been brought up on a diet of the boot and the fist. He tends to dislike all women as he internalised the message that you get what you want fast by using violence. At no time do you get it faster than when you lay into your defenceless woman in the privacy of your own home. Dinner not ready? Throw it in the air and punch her in the face. She doesn't feel like sex? Screw her anyway. How

45

does it make him feel? Good while he's doing it and bad when it's over.

The thoughts of a violent man are expressed in a letter sent to me by a man who used to batter his wife. He sent me this letter after seeing a film on the Refuge:

'I heard my wife speak with many voices during your programme. Each time re-emphasised for me the shame and remorse which I used to experience *after* the madness of an incident of violence: the renewed determination of "never again". My sense of compassion or wisdom used to black out and die in an explosion of frustraton in the moment *before* the blow was struck, just as her compassion and wisdom must have died in the moment of final provocation. What made it so reprehensible was that we were otherwise two 'normal', fairly rational and reasonable persons and apparently each capable of expressing ourselves, understanding and getting on well with almost anyone on earth except, sometimes (and not even the most *important* times!), each other.

'Our three children are now scattered and unsure where "home" really lies, although, except for our youngest who is fifteen, the elder two are fortunately old enough and mature enough to be leading their own lives and making their own careers and decisions. My wife (it's difficult to learn to precede "wife" with "ex" or "former"!) lives a kind of gypsy life in the hotel trade living in the company of another man. I live alone, very much withdrawn and with few visits from children and friends, with remembrances as punishments far more numerous than consolations. That I am deprived of making direct atonement is in itself the greatest punishment.

'Heart-failure in 1972 and two heart-attacks with three months in the hospital recently have warned me that I may be running out of time to do much or anything to try to make amends (agnostic, I can't even get religion!) and disablement benefit doesn't leave much cash to afford charitable gifts. On the other hand, I cannot afford *not* to send a pound to help you because it is the behaviour of men like me who cause the need for your work, and even though I know that a

46

million pounds cannot compensate for one blow struck or ever properly say "I'm sorry", still, I think you will understand what I'm trying to do and why.

'You will probably also understand why it was last September which brought my wife racing from —— to my hospital in —— to see me when my "clock" almost stopped. I think she feels no cause to *fear* me now; just a special kind of friendship and, I hope, some forgiveness. Selfishly, I hope she has not seen or may hear of your programme. For her it could only serve to revive memories which I would wish her to forget.

Yours very sincerely,'

He later wrote to me, 'One single act of violence is as damaging, creates as much lasting fear, impresses a watching child, as a hundred years of repetitive acts.' These men usually do end up alone and regretful. Many become dossers when they run out of women to look after them. It's amazing how many ex-solicitors, doctors and accountants huddle together down in Spitalfields. Most of their wives, unfortunately, have been long since abandoned by their children who tired of the war.

The second type, 'Mummy's boy', is pure mind-rot. Most of his damage is psychological. He has been emotionally incestuously seduced and spoiled. This is the man that is most difficult to have. At least where the violence is obvious, brutal and open, the woman can get away with her body damaged but her soul intact. The woman I dread – because I know how much work it will take to make her whole again – is the woman who has been completely destroyed mentally by a man so wedded to his mother that even death will not part them. It is an unholy alliance and the woman has no chance.

Unfortunately, this is the man who will present himself as the prince. And why not? This is how he has been brought up. His father is either absent or so ineffectual that the only reminder that he exists is his carpet slippers. Any woman looking at a man's family for the first time must look very carefully at his relationship with his mother. So many women believe that if he loves his mother he will love his wife. If he has to contact his mother all the time, stay away. If he constantly refers to her cooking, throw him out. If he talks all the time about how good she is at flower-arranging, housework, looking after him – leave immediately.

The prince gets his feet under another woman's table very quickly. Usually, he's quite comfortable at home, but you can't screw your mother, so he moves in with the next best thing he can find, and proceeds to make her life hell. It will take a long time before she realises it is not that she is mad, bad, frigid and lesbian. For many women, it is frightening to know that they have come to see me when it is too late. They come after years of trying to hold on to their own sanity.

'Fifteen years ago, I was at last free from the cruelty when he was asked to leave the house for a period while court proceedings progressed. I was not believed. When proof was desired it was changed round that I was at fault and asked for it. It was changed round that I was mentally ill as such that if I screamed, he said, I screamed so he hit me to stop me but this was not so. I screamed *because* he hit me.'

'A woman, a dog and a walnut tree – the more you beat them the better they be,' says the old English proverb. 'The farmer beats his wife,' the children sing as they dance round in a circle. Andy Capp cartoons. Jokes about violence to women. Films assuring us it's all right: women like it.

Finally here is the voice of woman in a refuge (and, God knows, refuges are places only for the very desperate):

'To those who are still suspicious of women who leave their husbands, bringing their often crying, noisy children with them, lowering the tone of the neighbourhood and putting more strain on the council and the taxpayer, we say this: we didn't all deserve everything we got (honestly, it was said) and we didn't leave our homes and friends from choice.

'We left for the most part, because our lives and our children's lives were very often in danger and so was our sanity. We left without a change of clothing, without a penny in our purses, indeed often without purses at all, and we left feeling so desperate that we did not even care where we were going. We needed safety, time to think, time to

48

re-organise our lives, and practical help, and all these things we got from the refuge.'

If you have a man you love, but you feel uneasy because he does one of the three following things or worse still, read *Scream Quietly, or the Neighbours Will Hear*, and then seek advice.

(1) He lashes out physically. He attacks verbally unreasonably.
(2) He is jealous without cause.
(3) He comes from a violent background or he is spoiled.

You ignore my warnings at your own peril. However, falling in love is aptly described by the Japanese as the 'divine madness'. So if your heart rules your head, and you wake up one day and discover you are living with a violent man, there is always a bed for you at the Refuge.

(Originally published January 1981, as 'Violence comes in pin-stripes too', reprinted by kind permission of *Cosmopolitan* magazine)

IN PRAISE OF YOUNGER MEN

'In praise of younger men' was a very prophetic piece. Three years later, I was to marry Jeff, who is twenty-one years younger than I am! The gigolo remark actually occurred and gave me the anger I needed to sit down and write an article in defence of the woman that walked past our table.

A male acquaintance of mine was sitting in a restaurant with me when an obviously much younger man strolled past us with an attractive middle-aged lady on his arm. 'Gigolo,' he said with such venom I raised my eyebrows and tipped my hot soup into his lap. Why, I asked outraged, should it be considered disgusting for an older woman to have a lover considerably younger than herself and acceptable for an older man to escort a younger woman around town?

Nothing ends an evening more dramatically than a burnt foreskin so I retired home to consider the implications of such obvious prejudice. And I came to the conclusion that there was a major revolution unnoticed by social commentators. The time has come to whistle up the sociologists, psychiatrists, social services and indeed Parliament itself (given the involvement of the Royal Family) to examine in pleasurable detail the case for making it acceptable for older women to come out of the broom closet and face the light of day.

Elton John says if he had another relationship it would probably be with an older woman. John Travolta rejected his screaming millions of teeny-boppers for the love of a mature woman. There wouldn't have been so much publicity over Princess Margaret's relationship with Roddy had he not been younger. And most of the hounding was done by male reporters. On the other side of the fence, an international actress of seventy-nine said of her much younger husband, 'At my age you need a younger man.' Let us look at the benefits for a woman.

In the bad old days before the wind of change blew through the land and said it was OK to be yourself in spite of Persil, Vim and underarm deodorant, women feared the advent of a birthday or a sag, bag or wrinkle more than death itself. The 'dolly-bird' – the brainless, ever-smiling, subservient adolescent chick – was the sign of the Sixties. Men were judged by their ability to abuse and misuse a production line of ever-available Lolita-type women, and the clothes and fashion photographs of that time reinforced those prejudices until any woman over twenty-five buried her head in the sink and wept into the washing machine.

There were two roles: nymphet or wife-and-mother. Wife-and-mother stayed at home awaiting the arrival of the partner, who more often than not was escorting a girl young enough to be his daughter to the nearest fashionable watering hole. It never crossed the minds of women who were considered 'past it' (which meant they were over twenty-five) that they had any possibility of playing the field, because even if they were single or divorced, all available men of their age group were either married or hotfully pursuing the local Lolita. So the 'has-been' resigned herself to a life of servitude and was hailed as a saint when she would much rather have been a sinner.

In those days men competed to own a beautiful woman to match their cars, watches and bank accounts. What went on between the woman's ears was considerably less important than what they could boast about that went on between the legs. In fact the men of the Sixties and early Seventies didn't really like women very much at all.

Gradually, thanks a lot to the Women's Movement (if you forget for the moment those screaming harridans who ruined it for the broad mass of women), many of us began to vibrate to the injustice and outrage of an angry oppression and women began to get a feel of themselves. There were, for example, historic moments – epitomised by Katharine Whitehorn, who wrote an article liberating all hopelessly inadequate house-wives like myself, by confessing that she was an untidy, disorganised slut and didn't care. There was heady copy from Jill Tweedie that catapulted so many of us out of the prisons of our homes and made us meet other women in groups and share our experiences. There were women who insisted they needn't shave their arms and legs, could smell of themselves and face the world without false eyelashes, so that a whole new confidence filtered through to all women. And just now more and more women are turning away from relationships with men who have been trained by their time to appreciate only non-threatening 'little women' relationships, to choose partners among men who may be years younger but who are in fact much more mature in their ability to accept the kind of loving women can give.

Looking at a relationship with a younger man from an older woman's point of view, I've found it has many advantages. It has always been noted that a man is most sexually active in his early twenties and thereafter, given mortgages, a three-piece suite on H.P. and children, not surprisingly his performance diminishes. Women, it is sometimes whispered, like cheese and violins, improve with age. This is largely because once they have fulfilled their conditioned need to marry and bear children, they are free to enjoy sex as a pleasure rather than a biological drive. And given the state of the law today, which has swung like a pendulum until it is now grossly unfair to men, it has given the divorced woman her own property, the children and an income – with the freedom, then, to choose a man for pleasure and companionship rather than financial and biological need.

Indeed, as I look around at my contemporaries, I see more and more of them turning their backs on the unfulfilled males of their own age group, locked into the confines of their expectations of women, in favour of much younger men, who do not demand the traditional roles of women. A young man allows them to throw off the chains that bind them to the kitchen sink and the nappy bucket, and allows them the freedom to fulfil themselves as whole people in whatever role they choose to take without suffering a mortal wound to their male ego. Above all, given the independence and freedom which has been bitterly achieved by so many women, a relationship with a much younger man carries far less threat of the demand for permanence found so often in the desperation of a man in his forties and fifties fruitlessly wandering from one unsatisfactory marriage to another.

It is also true that most women involved in bringing up children are able to keep in touch with the child within themselves, whereas the men in those marriages are debarred, given the society we live in, from much of the playing that goes on in the mother-child relationship. And the woman can find in a younger partner the ability to revitalise this childish and playful part of herself quite unselfconsciously, and thereby benefit immensely by regaining a lost part of her personality.

Of course there are great insecurities in a relationship with much younger men. A woman is always afraid that he may find a younger, more attractive girl than herself. But talking this through with a lot of women friends, the consensus was that a relationship was a relationship and could break for any number of reasons. Security in the relationship came from throwing away the concept of age limits and relaxing in the love of another human being.

It can be confidently said that now we can declare this is the era of the older woman. Just compare the Fifties and Sixties and the starlets of those days – Brigitte Bardot, Jean Shrimpton, Twiggy et al. – with today, when even the major film stars are in their thirties or early forties like Jane Fonda, Ali MacGraw and Lee Remick.

Most women are now able to accept themselves just as they are, without the need for a face-lift or roll-on. And if they bulge, or wrinkle a little, well, those are honourable scars of a life fully lived rather than a sign of doom and despair. Women age physically more quickly than most men, but not emotionally. So it seems quite natural that finding younger partners should be the prerogative of both sexes rather than seen as victory by men and an unacceptable aberration in a woman.

From the younger man's point of view, I can do no better than quote a certain bachelor of thirty, or thereabouts, who reported to me in an amazed voice that most of his bachelor friends were going around positively moist-eyed about middle-aged women with children – 'moving in droves', he said.

Without sounding at all cynical or anti-male, just routinely suspicious, I must point out that living with an older woman bears certain financial advantages. He doesn't have to keep her – and why should he in these liberated days? He doesn't have to pay the mortgage, since some other poor fellow does that. He can enjoy the children, love them and play with them, but they aren't his responsibility and he doesn't have the threat of marriage looming over his head.

What he can give is uncomplicated loving warmth and a sense of fun. Emotionally he can find time to mature in her arms and she can blossom again, perhaps after years of drudgery. These relationships probably don't last – though sometimes they do. But for those unattached people who are free to make new relationships, there's a lot to be said for it, judging by the amount of people giving it a try.

I shall shortly be moving to Suffolk, so after re-reading this article I have decided that I rather fancy the idea of a young farmer with dirt under his nails. My dislike of any form of exercise, other than floating about in hot baths soaking in bath oil and drinking iced champagne, is well known, so I shall hire myself a helicopter on Saturdays and swoop through the fields. Suffolk farmers, you have been warned.

(Originally published March 1979, as 'Catch 'em young', reprinted by kind permission of *Cosmopolitan* magazine)

A LITTLE BIT ON THE SIDE

As I say in this article, I was absolutely bewildered at how few couples I knew who even attempted to be faithful to each other. I suppose it's like most things. If you're faithful, you tend to assume everyone else is unless someone rubs your nose in it. I think I was trying yet again to understand why men and women weren't on the whole very happy with one another.

> *'Higamous hogamous woman is monogamous.*
> *Hogamous higamous man is polygamous.'*

Well, there you have it in two sentences. I think it was written by that well-known philosopher 'Anon'. However, I don't think anyone could have put the whole matter more succinctly. Some men lust their hearts away, but others give in almost immediately at any opportunity. Men are by nature hunters. These days they can't go out steeling moose but have to make do with snaring the office typist.

For so many men the chase is the excitement, and that is why somebody woke up several hundred years ago and said, *'Post coitum omne animale triste est'*, which loosely translated, means: Now I have had the office typist she's gone off her shorthand and I've gone off the whole idea. There is a huge distinction between sex and relationships which include sex. This is where so many men and women come unstuck. The old saying that love is everything to a woman but to a man is a thing apart is true. Straightforward sexual encounters, commonly known as one-night stands, are no problem for a man, but even the most ardent feminist I know will swear she feels the same though usually she is sitting hunched over the phone.

When I lived in Macao I watched Ho Yin, who was a local

Chinese millionaire, run his household. He had four wives in four different houses in one compound. His first wife was the senior wife and there was no doubt that he loved her the best. He was kind to all four, and to my naïve eyes it worked well. I often visited them, and they shared their kids and all the duties, including him, with a remarkable lack of jealousy or resentment. Of course you could argue that they were conditioned to accept the situation. On the other hand, who ever conditioned us to have and to stranglehold one other human being for the odd fifty years?

The other time I watched seemingly happy relationships was on a Greek island, where the women again have a very strong sense of self. They have a life of sharing with other women in their extended families and an almost casual relationship with their partners. There the morality is very strict. The men as usual can mess about, but only with 'tourist' women.

On my arrival I saw a Greek man from another island whom the villagers had caught after he had seduced a friend's wife. They shaved his head, stoned him and left him for dead. I hate to think what they did to her.

All through history men have always been more lightly punished for philandering than women. I had a very tense month because I had three eighteen-year-old boys camping with me. They lit up at the sight of the very pretty Greek girls, but I soon pointed out the Greek men minus arms or legs and said it was quite a price to pay. They didn't find out till the end of the holiday that it was dynamiting fish that had caused the loss of limb.

Every year at the festival in August part of the occasion is the young virgins' march from deep down the one main road with their hands behind their backs to show off their figures. The young men watch reverently because these will be the wives of the future. Of course, once they marry they join another huge extended family and the women are the matriarchs and the men peripheral.

I have often wondered if women organised themselves better and had more interesting and interacting life styles that didn't depend on 'what did you do today darling?', or were not limited to dull jobs because we are second-rate citizens, if men would be more inclined to be faithful. There is nothing to be said for a sex life during the time a woman is bringing up children. During that time she is just a tired, boring machine. Sex is usually nothing more than 'keeping him happy'; so many women I talk to say that's when they organise the next day's shopping or make a laundry list. It is obvious that a day full of dirty nappies, fish-fingers and snot does not pass into an evening of lustful orgiastic sex.

I like the joke where the gorilla is pulling a woman lustfully through the bars of his cage and she calls out to her husband for help. He says calmly, 'tell him you've got one of your head-aches.' It's cruel but true. They want a virgin/whore/cordon-bleu cook/mother/childcare officer/secretary, all in one woman. When women organise together they can fulfil many functions, or those that they wish. But while they live isolated lives channelled only through men they have no chance but to be a captive, and once captured most men start to wander.

It isn't till you get divorced that the scales fall from your eyes and you realise that all those happily married couples that you shared your life with have actually been sharing each other's beds. It comes as something of a shock to a nicely brought up convent school girl, but over the last few years I have been taking stock of the situation and here is my decidedly female run-down on the polygamous male. I must say right now that I know women who screw like rattlesnakes, but there are male writers who can comment on their activities. For the moment I shall examine the predatory male and how he operates.

Michael is my classic example of so many men that I know. He has been married for ten years and has a homely wife on an estate in an outer London suburb. They have three children, and Michael married when he was twenty-three really because she wanted to and most of his friends were getting married. Jenny took to marriage like a duck to water. She was a good cook, good fun, sexy and adventurous, but after the first child Michael found that fatherhood was a put-up job to shackle him to the house, and took to going off to the pub leaving her with the baby.

There was a girl in the pub who often dropped in for a drink on her way home, and one day he went over and spoke to her. She was very friendly, lived nearby, gave him her address and said 'drop by if you feel like it and I'll give you dinner.' Michael lit up like an electric torch. He didn't tell her he was married but took himself off home with a gleam in his eye that surprised his wife and surprised her even further when he was unusually amorous in bed. Michael wrestled with his conscience for a few days, but lust won and he telephoned her and made arrangements to have dinner. The day dawned as usual except that Michael spent an awful long time in the bathroom, put on his best suit, changed ties about six times and did more press-ups than usual. Jennifer understood it was because he'd been invited out to dinner with the boss and his wife. She saw him off very proudly at the front door and congratulated herself on their happy marriage.

Men in a high state of arousal all day have different physical problems to women. Michael spent most of the day with a newspaper at hand. He rehearsed the 'Hello', thought about the dinner and then wondered what next. He felt quite worn out by the time he arrived at her flat clutching a bottle of chilled white wine. He was terrified. What if she turned out to have no teeth and the blonde hair had been a wig? Worse still, what if she had an eighteen-stone boyfriend who didn't like white wine? He knocked, and it took several heart attacks before the door opened and she was just as he remembered. The light shone on her golden hair, she smiled and her teeth were reassuringly her own. She put out her hand and led him into the sitting room, where the table was laid for two. It looked as though similar thought had been given to the bed-room.

They had a marvellous dinner. She hung on his every word. She was a bachelor girl, well paid and she enjoyed her freedom. It seemed perfectly natural after three bottles of wine and several brandies to move to the bedroom and lie there making contented noises. Not much passed through Michael's mind at that moment because he was busy with buttons and belts. He did wonder if she took the pill but he didn't like to ask. It was far too late anyway. They made love and fell asleep until Michael woke with a start realising it was daybreak. She looked lovely asleep but he knew he was already in trouble. He woke her to say he must go and she hugged him and said, 'you will come again won't you?' Every part of him said yes except his conscience, which stabbed him in the back – 'adulterer'. He walked home in the dawn light checking his clothes for fair hair and frantically thinking of excuses for not contacting Jennifer, and feeling guilty. However, she understood why he didn't phone. She had cried a bit because she was so worried but she was happy to have him back. He tottered upstairs just as the children rushed to him, covering him with their kisses, one with the contents of a smelly nappy.

Michael grew more successful. Jennifer grew quieter and more motherly. Michael soon worked all week in London and spent Friday night to Sunday at home. Michael had his social life organised around three or four girls whom he would wine and dine and then bed. Most of his waking time was devoted to the Walter Mitty style of seeing that no one knew about anybody else. They all knew he was married. They all professed they would *never* marry. But the excitement of the game was in the planning and the organising. Being an insurance agent may be a piece of cake but running a harem was quite another. His technique became expert. He ceased to have to take them out to dinner by convincing them that all we wanted to do was to curl up in their flat, so his contribution was a bottle of wine and theirs was dinner and bed.

Michael was a very typical example of a man who found most of his excitement in the chase. He had no deep feelings for the women. If they began to cling he'd move on. The sex wasn't that important – it was more like a sneeze below the belt. It was really his ego that needed flattering, and unless he got caught out he would remain a philanderer until he was too old to pull the birds. His wife might find out, in which case he'd promise to reform (for a while) or, if she really recognised the immaturity of his character, she'd throw him out. Most women choose to stay married to these men rather than go it alone. You can always pick them out if they get invited to the office party because they stand against the wall clutching a glass of sherry in one hand, trying hard to be invisible.

There is one of nature's huge jokes around for promiscuous men. Now all women have their own contraceptives men can no longer protect themselves with sheaths from nasty little bugs like NSU, which is carried by the female without any symptoms but is very uncomfortable for the male. Herpes is another of nature's jokes. They feel like cigarette burns and the man can get them *anywhere*. A quick check at your local VD clinic can be quite a laugh as your next door neighbour hides behind the *Guardian*. *The Times* readers are not immune, I must add, but they tend to go 'private'.

Much more cosy and reliable is the one-mistress man, but it's much more dangerous. Here a man finds a lonely woman and seduces her, or she may well seduce him. They end up promising each other that there is only true love but no wish to possess on either side. He has a perfectly amiable wife and life-style and has no intention of changing it. She, however, in spite of the independent pitch, has every intention of getting him hooked. It takes a year or two before she begins to get aggressive if he spends time away. He reminds her of their promise. She then takes to ringing up the house to hear the wife's voice. She starts lurking round the house until she sees the wife and the children. Slowly and insidiously she manoeuvres herself into his family. Then one day she shows up on the wife's doorstep and tells. Sometimes it works.

It's not the sex that ruins the marriage but the lying and the cheating. Many wives would forgive their men but for the fact that they could never trust them again. Many men learn when their wives turn them out that very often a mistress doesn't make a good wife. There are liaisons that go quietly on for years and no one knows until she turns up at the funeral, but usually the 'other woman' is out to get the man. Here again, the man just likes to have his cake and eat it, with the result that he gets chronic indigestion.

The wife who sits at home never suspecting is not at all rare. I have heard so many women say, 'my husband would never have an affair without telling me' – those men are the ones that usually are. Women are conditioned to the fact that men have the freedom to come and go, stay late at the office, have a social life that ignores them, and once they become housebound they accept the stories and lies. Also those back-breaking years of bringing up small children dull the senses to cabbage-like proportions. The interesting thing about these wives is that in the last few years as their husbands have played around, the wives are far more likely to get rid of them and make a life of their own.

The other way of dealing with it is to accept that men, like cats, roam and come home when they feel like it. I have a friend who swears it is the only way to have a good relationship with her husband. She makes no attempt to domesticate him. She just lets him loose. I notice he's more around her house than most husbands.

Lenny Bruce, whose tongue was as sharp as his heroin needle, once remarked that the trouble with women is that they are always looking for a relationship with a woman through a man. The fact is men are not at all like women emotionally and it is no good expecting them to behave like your compassionate, intuitive girlfriends. A man will be caring in his own way as long as the F.A. Cup isn't on.

Recently I was in America, where everyone was into 'open relationships'. Well, the first time I discussed a couple's open relationship, he looked like a fat cat, while she was anorexic and hysterical. Both of them sang the joys of a bit on the side and the pleasure of being back again. When he left for the night she sobbed all over me . . . 'How the hell am I going to have a lover with three small babies?' she howled. Anyway, she didn't want to have affairs. The second couple was the reverse. She was a dynamic, pneumatic blonde and he was awfully ugly. I listened yet again to how well it all worked. It did for her. She gave me an invaluable tip: 'Conferences,' she said, 'is where it all happens.' I was fascinated. I've always wondered why people go to draughty halls and eat cafeteria food. Now I know. Anyway, he was so unsuccessful that he shot himself. She was furious with him.

There are no easy answers to relationships, except perhaps to say that honesty should be the binding pact between partners. If you are involved with a man who finds it necessary to have illicit, furtive passion on the side, there is little point in hanging about unless you are prepared to put up with it. He is usually sexually damaged and it is the illicit 'naughty boy' syndrome that gives him the kicks. He is the sort of man who keeps his drawers at work full of presents from his lady lovers – Turnbull & Asser shirts, the odd gold chain and other mementos. I saw one man get his come-uppance the other day when he left his mistress. He was the one-mistress type. Unfortunately he had no sense of smell at all. His lady love was fed up with the scene so she sprayed his suit liberally with Jolie Madame. As it was an afternoon session he walked home with the evening paper under one arm, swinging his brolly with a sense of well-being. His wife opened the door and was hit with a blast of perfume that was not hers. He confessed. He is now living in his mistress's bedsit and she is fast going off him. There is nothing sadder than a man whose wife finally *does* understand him.

(Originally published April 1980, as 'The roaming male', reprinted by kind permission of *Cosmopolitan* magazine)

LAMENT OF A LOVELY
ROUNDED LADY

This poem was written many years ago. It was at a time when I had just come to London with my family. My first husband got a job with the BBC and I was meeting 'smart' people. That meant thin people. I went home after a dinner party where I was the only woman at the table to have potatoes and the pudding. I think the poem was to comfort myself.

Everyone wants to stroke me,
    cajole and bespoke me,
        but I'd rather wander and in solitude ponder
            the dimensions of grandure
                as seen in the panda
                    and then I'd expire
                        to the strains of a lyre.

        Nobody'd wish for a moribund dish,
            and in the grasp of a grave
                no approval I'd win
                    so I'd lie in the dark and
                        I'd grin and
                            I'd grin.

FABULOUSLY FAT

The following article appeared in *Cosmopolitan* eighteen years later.

If you cough you'll be told it's because you're fat. If you laugh they'll tell you all fat people are jolly. If you are depressed they'll tell you it's because you are too fat. In fact anyone who doesn't look on the verge of anorexia is subject to millions of pounds of emotional blackmail.

The worse enemy of the whole conspiracy is other women. Seventy per cent of greetings between women start with a comment on whether or not one has put on or taken off weight followed by a long discussion on diets. Who has not had to sit next to something resembling a garden rake at dinner and watch her chase a limp piece of lettuce round her plate, making you feel positively porcine as you nosh your way through NW1 goulash.

However, I detect a change in the air. Just recently there was a report in the *Daily Mirror* where they had done a survey asking men whether they liked women fat or thin. I am delighted to tell you that the fatties did best. But why or how did it ever get to a situation when to be fat actually meant that many women suffered serious emotional damage or feelings of dislike for themselves and an emotional round of crash dieting followed by midnight binges that very nearly destroyed their lives?

Fat women went out of fashion in a big way when photographers and fashion designers took the brushes out of the hands of artists. Now, most artists like women in all shapes, forms and sizes, especially in the Rubens era, when they were huge, rosy and smiling. Rubens knew a lot about women as well and it was his advice to all women that the best sexual exercise available to all was scrubbing the floor with a scrubbing brush – which may well be why their bottoms are rosy with exertion and could lead to a whole new line of make up. Of course those who take language seriously now know where the term 'scrubber' came from.

However, back to the serious subject of the conspiracy. People like photographers or fashion designers – who decided to dictate what a fashionable woman should look like are not in the business of human relations but in the business of showing off clothes which actually need clothes-horses, or photo-graphers who are usually so insecure that they lead a vicarious life hidden behind their camera lens and only relate to women so faint with hunger and malnutrition that they are unable to be any kind of threat.

It only took a short time for the media and manufacturing market to decide that here was a huge national neurosis that could be turned into a multi-million pound business and the whole 'make them guilty' act went into full swing.

The secret of being fat and feeling fabulous is that you spend a long time actually talking to yourself about the advantages and disadvantages of being fat or not. I started with the advantages. First of all, was I prepared with my genetic back-ground of huge Irish potato diggers prepared to live on a diet of lettuce, no alcohol and a climax of a lean piece of meat once a week. I imagined the effect it would have on my love life as I lay in the arms of some romantic lover muttering sweet nothings in my ear would be was that all I could think of was a pound of rare steak and it's a pity it's only Wednesday. No, I was not prepared to diet to that extent and any other extent meant that I would not fit into the normal weight range. If I was going to be outsize, I might as well indulge in anything I liked to eat and drink, and just accept the size I am, enjoying the good things about it – like the fact that you can terrorise everybody because the sight of a large, angry woman maketh even the most outraged male feel quite faint. Or you can use the other warm, maternal side which cuddles and loves all things great and small and naturally they come your way for love and protection, so you're never short of friends.

Most fat people have beautiful skin and age very slowly because the fat under the skin stops wrinkles. It's nice not to suffer from spots and to know that your skin is soft and silky compared to your best friend who lives on vinegar and whose skin feels like rhino hide but looks just great in a leotard. Because I was always fat my mother would look at my twin sister with great pride and predict a glowing future for her, while adding that I wasn't to worry as I had 'character'. I decided that 'having character' was going to be a very positive asset and they have been trying to lock me up ever since.

Fat women usually have nice large breasts which fashion has made them so self-conscious that they wear horrible punitive machines from awful places like Evans Outsizes, which always reminds me of a fatties remand centre. I decided either to have nice comfortable bras made or not to wear one at all. Lots of men love women with large breasts, and I must admit I did discover a sharp kick on the shin dissuades gropers.

On the subject of men, which is where most women believe they need their bones to protrude from their ribs, I must say that it is usually very insecurely sexed men, or men who are latently homosexual and can only relate to an androgynous female, that shy away from fat women. On the whole fat ladies are very cuddly and I have never felt my size to be a disadvantage. The only disadvantage is finding a man who is not totally narcissistic or, although six foot, makes me feel I'm dealing with a small boy.

Obviously if you have spent all your life looking at pictures of women with anonymously regular bodies, the idea of stripping off in front of the love of your life is not actually easy. There are various approaches like climbing into the wardrobe and coming out with a flannel nightie buttoned from the chin down to the feet. There is the 'night flying' approach which is to say that you are just going to tidy up – and get him to go ahead and get into bed. You then strip off in the loo, charge into the bedroom, switch off the light and make a crash landing on the spot where you hope he is not. If he is, you might be arrested, and under the circumstances – as one might put it – you would probably get off with manslaughter or, if the judge had a sense of humour, 'parking in an occupied zone'.

But as I said I just believe that if you are going to accept that you are going to be fat then both those approaches only prove that you haven't really come to terms with your size and the proper answer is to have really pretty nighties. I get old Victorian cotton nighties from a stall at Portobello market. They are lovely, fresh and enveloping and slowly you can gain confidence that whoever you are with will love you warts and all, bearing in mind that most lovers are not in the slightest bit worried about the other's imperfections, only their own. Along with liking yourself the way you are, it follows that you begin to take care of your hair and make up if you want to wear any. Most fat women have big, strong faces that take make up very well. It's fun to use kohl round your eyes and paint on a wide canvas. Get some good advice from someone like Mary Quant and wear her stuff; you can afford to be different and outstanding because nature made you that way.

On the subject of clothes in general you can only join my club by boycotting places like Evans Outsizes. There is no need to go there and feel dreadful. The shops are now full of excellent clothes that can really only be worn by big women.

I very often wander round maternity shops, too. Once you like your size and decide to enjoy it, then buying clothes becomes fun, not a terribly embarrassing business because the shop assistant looks at you as though you have a bad disease. It becomes a pleasure when you know where to go to find clothes that will fit anyone, and that you won't return home empty-handed and miserable.

I often go up to Shepherd's Bush market where they have the most beautiful Indian materials – anything from a glowing sari shot with gold to beautiful batik prints. I also enjoy jostling among the market stalls with the West Indian women, many of whom are as large as me and don't ever give it a thought. I must admit, though, that black fat is more beautiful than white fat. Next time round I want to be a Jamaican. Anyway, I buy enough to go round me, take it home and lay it on the floor doubled over into a square. I then cut straight up from the bottom to where I want the sleeves to be, and cut out one arm and then up the other side – and I have the outlines of a kaftan. I then make the neck into a 'V'. After a while I got very sophisticated and when I got to running up the sides with my machine I put in two darts from the sides to where I hoped my nipples would be. I had a bad time getting it right, but like everything else it comes with practice and I can make a sensational dress for very little money in an afternoon. You can line the neck with anything from soft fur to feathers. I gave up feathers because they made me sneeze and blew my false eyelashes into my gin. I gave up gin because it makes me tell the truth, the whole truth and nothing but the truth – which tends to empty rooms and lose one friends.

Along with being large I like large things. It is much better to have a big car however old than crush oneself into a Mini. I have a Great Dane called Morgan who makes me feel very insignificant. I didn't realise how large they grew and it seemed like a good idea at the time.

As you get used to the idea of how special and unusual you are you can have fun practising grand entrances into restaurants – sweeping into the middle of the room, do a half turn and enjoy everyone looking at you. Watch out that you get it right or your partner may be found unconscious in the far corner and you will have to pay the bill. Thank God for the National Health – you can afford a few mistakes. You will never be denied a table. The last owner who said he was full changed his mind when I said I was paralysed with sorrow and he would have to carry me out himself. Rather than die of a coronary in front of his spell-bound audience he found us seats.

If you are very large, a very long cigarette-holder looks quite natural and indeed gives one an undisputed authority. Should anyone disagree with you, you can make your point very hotly felt with a quick jab in their direction. All of it is fun. Like all of yourself all the way round – even if it takes a wall-to-wall mirror – and you will enjoy life.

So far I've looked at the positive side. The negative side doesn't take long. Other women are my biggest problem. They run up to me with their little anxious faces asking, 'Why don't you diet?' 'Because I don't want to,' I say amiably. This usually sends them off into a frenzy. It is interesting, if I ever watch old interviews on the work I do at Chiswick, to see how women journalists go on at great length on how big I am and what I am wearing. Whereas male journalists get on with the job of talking about the mothers and kids. I do waste a lot of time defending myself over my utter lack of shame at not being the same size as everybody else – not really for my own benefit, but for all those beautiful put-down women who need to know that they can love and be loved and that attraction is not a physical thing. It is very mystical and comes from one warm loving human being to another.

Finally, here comes the government health warning bit. Fat makes you have blood-pressure. Well – as Dr Nixon, who knows more about these matters than anyone else I know, points out – there are as many thinnies as fatties running around with high blood-pressure. You won't live as long as a skinny. I don't want to if I have to give up all the things I like.

A closing thought: the subject of exercise. Like many fat people I am very supple so I don't feel much actual need for exercise. Lately there has been this jogging craze, and I look out of my window and watch the red-faced puffing joggers go by. And I reflect that it is apparently a fact that an orgasm uses the same amount of energy as a five-mile run. So take your pick.

(Originally published February 1980, as 'Fat and fabulous', reprinted by kind permission of *Cosmopolitan* magazine)

CHRISTMAS COMES BUT ONCE A YEAR

One of the plusses of separating is being able to order your own life. This piece about Christmas was a hymn of joy to my liberation from Christmases past.

I had such awful Christmases as a child, either standing in lines in one institution or another or with my warring parents, that I have a totally self-indulgent childish need to have the best Christmas I ever had each year. When I talk to people about their Christmas I am always amazed at how many of them say that they remember a tense, angry, sad Christmas at home when the family and relations gathered for what should have been a happy event and it turned out just the opposite.

At this time of year people gather together to celebrate the sacred moment of the birth of Christ and the beautiful story of the nativity, which has deep mythological and symbolic significance throughout all religions. Instead of celebrating it, the occasion is usually fraught with competition. It is also financially, physically and emotionally a strain.

I decided that once I was a single parent I would never work my fingers to the bone keeping up with the Joneses, the Smiths *et al*. Nor would I allow anyone I didn't love to enter the house and destroy the happiness of our Christmas.

This rudely shocked several people who had invaded us for years. It also meant declining standard invitations to other people's houses. To spend Christmas Day going from one set of people to another getting slowly plastered and then home to produce the biggest meal of the year seemed a terrible travesty of what I felt Christmas was about. The few Christmases I've spent as a captive in other people's houses convinced me that the sight of the ladies of the house rising from their beds at ghostly dawn to bang about in the kitchen 'getting the turkey started', and incidentally waking up the rest of the family, guests, cats and dogs, only started the day on a good guilt trip.

I remember lying in bed staring at the ceiling hissing obscenities at one particular matriarch called June, who not only rose at cock-crow but insisted that all females in the house joined her. Not me; I stayed put. However, the rest of the day was a nightmare. When I did finally rise and grace the breakfast table I saw two fried eggs staring unbelievably at me. Anyone who enjoys a bibulous Christmas Eve knows that breakfast should properly consist of Andrew's Liver Salts to clear the system for the day's gastronomic onslaught and a large does of vitamin C to nurse the body back to health.

I was very sick. They were amazed, and I had to lie down while she had to clear up. Fortunately martyrs love clearing up. The rest of the morning was taken up with friends and neighbours dropping by talking about their parents, what they were going to eat and how much it all cost. The Christmas meal was served at 3 p.m., by which time a miasma of turkey grease, stewing vegetables and mountains of china and cutlery seemed to envelop the women trying to cope with it all.

In the kitchen steam from the pressure cooker billowed about the matriarch's head as she issued a series of contradictory orders to the platoon. I was detailed to 'Lay the Table'. It sounded as important a task as being born or dying. Unfortunately, I don't know my left from my right so I did my best.

Finally the troops marched in and everyone sat down in an exhausted silence. Pandemonium broke out when they discovered the chaos of the place settings. The matriarch behaved as though I had been rude to the Queen.

Then followed the opening of the family presents. It was highly entertaining as all the men were given after-shave by the women, and the men gave the women Boots assorted bath cubes. The matriarch did the carving while Daddy sat at the head of the table pretending he was very manly. All the men were served first. Only they got the dark meat and we, being delicate females, got the white. Three veg, three kinds of stuffing, ham, roast and boiled potatoes, followed by home-made Christmas pudding, brandy butter without much brandy, mince pies, fruit and nuts. Whoever invented the Christmas menu was a sadist, and all those who eat it, unless it is excellently cooked, are masochists.

The only way of coping with that particular Christmas Day was oblivion, so I went back to bed. The men washed up while the women made jokes about Women's Lib and put everything away neatly, because you can't trust men with important jobs like that. 'Never again,' I said to myself. If that was a family Christmas, give me institutions anytime. Scrooge obviously knew a thing or two.

That's what I thought Christmas was about until I discovered my own. I have had three Christmases at home surrounded by my children, adopted family and friends. This Christmas will follow the same pattern, and I will await Christmas 1981 with the same excitement.

First of all I love all the tradition that goes with Christmas. There is the collecting of holly from the holly tree at Bristol Women's Aid. Sometimes there are mothers and children who stay with me for Christmas. We also look for mistletoe to hang inside the front door. If I can't find it – one has to look for it wrapped round old apple trees – I buy it. Mistletoe is very magic, apart from the fun of all the kissing. I love the wreath of holly and ivy which I try and make. It doesn't last long because someone always nicks it from the front door. Amos (my son) sprays all the windows with supposedly artistic snow scenes. It gives a lovely frosted look to the house but takes at least a year to get off.

Last year's decorations are brought out about a week before 'The Day'. The tree with roots, so that I don't feel guilty, is bought from a gardening centre and Russ, one of my adopted sons, wires it up. There is always an argument about whether he will blow up the house or fuse all the lights. For several hours he fiddles around and finally they come on. The look of joy on my grandchildren's faces at this momentous occasion in their little lives is well worth the overdraft. I love Christmas lights – huge, vulgar ones that flash in sequence. Both the cats find the tree enchanting. We take it in turns to patrol the stairs as the cats make a Rousseau-like painting and lurk inside the tree grinning hugely as we try and shoo them out. Every so often they get so carried away chasing each other round the branches that there is a terrible crash, and the tree ends up on the floor with the cats walking away with their tails like lavatory brushes, pretending they had nothing to do with it.

The tree decorations are a kaleidoscope of green and gold and silver with ropes of tinsel and lots of bits of cotton wool pretending to be snow flakes. 'Oh Mum,' says Cleo (my daughter). All week we get out all the presents we have collected for everyone coming for Christmas Day. Cleo is excellent at wrapping things, so we ban various members of the resident tribe while we do up their presents. I do my share but I hate wrapping things, so I use tin foil and add a pretty butterfly from a shop called Paper Chase to make it look as if I'd tried.

I don't send Christmas cards because I need the money for presents for the many children who will come that day, but fortunately lots of my old mothers and children send me cards, and they hang on strings or shelves cheerfully.

Amos is dreadful and sneaks around all week checking on who's getting what. He keeps saying he wants money not presents, but I insist – and then we compromise. I buy him the records he wants, which involves hanging out in a totally West Indian reggae shop feeling like an idiot. I'm surrounded by Rastafarians trying to ask for a record, which comes decorated with large cigarette-shaped objects containing dubious substances.

Amos is deeply committed to Rastafarianism and believes that when the boat arrives to rescue the faithful he will have a reserved seat. We Babylonians will be washed away in the ensuing floods. He does, however, offer hope if one allows him to lie in bed, eat the fridge clean and avoid washing up.

By Christmas Eve the feeling of excitement is at fever pitch. The table in the sitting room is groaning with Special Brew, wine and mince pies. I buy my mince pies and my sister makes hers. They both taste great because I drown them with brandy.

After leaving the refuge with the children and mothers getting ready for the next day I prepare for Christmas Eve, when everyone I love drops by and anyone we don't love gets moved off by Russ. Soon the basement is packed with people and the music is shaking the foundations. Everyone is dancing.

At half-past eleven I leave with as many people who want to go to church in St Peter's Square. Usually we are a motley crew of assorted nationalities, but our wish is sincere. For me the midnight service epitomises all that is real about the festival of Christmas. The joy of people uniting to celebrate the birth of a life given, and the moment when we all stream out into the night kissing each other and wishing strangers a Merry Christmas and a Happy New Year.

We all walk back to the house singing carols, and then it is time to put the two grandchildren to bed. A teaspoon of Actifed makes sure the little darlings don't rise at an uncivilised hour. If children get you up at 5 a.m. you are not very nice to them at 5 p.m., so I bury my guilt feelings at doping defenceless children and read them my favourite Christmas story: 'It was the night before Christmas when all through the house . . .' They wait until I've fallen asleep half-way through and get back to the party.

Trevor (another adopted son) is the major domo of the house. He comes into his own on Christmas Day. It was a tribal vote that we use paper plates and paper cups because we all want to watch all the old movies and no one wants to wash up – certainly not for an army. So we have red cups and plates and gold foil over the tables. Those that don't get a seat sit on the floor. The cooking is done by everyone.

We have a very simple Christmas dinner. The turkey is a fresh one, and with deference to the West Indian members of the family, it is well garlicked and rubbed with curry powder and peanut butter. I put it in the oven at lunch time and cook it fast until six or seven. We have a bought ham, and our local baker makes very good Christmas puds. Actually we do as much as possible to keep the work to a minimum and the pleasure to the maximum. Trevor sees that we all get everything together when we should. I join the rest of the staff in the refuge during the day to see the mothers and kids. It is one of my happiest moments to know that my family extends to all those families and we are all enjoying Christmas, and especially those children who have never known 'peace on earth' in their little lives.

I come back and we get the last bits of assorted pickles, cranberry sauce and bread sauce (from a packet, made with lots of fresh herbs). Then we all sit down having loaded our plates from the kitchen. Usually Russ has dropped by at his local and brought someone home who looks a bit bemused at the sight but soon settles down and joins in.

The table looks lovely with my great extravagance, which is a £12 box of Harrods crackers. I justify buying them by saying they have such really nice presents in them, but actually it's the hats. We all pull crackers and swop jokes.

Then we eat the first course. During a pause we pull the 'party poppers' which cascade streamers all over the room. It is then the time for the triumph of the march of the Christmas pudding. In it comes in a blue blaze, which usually refuses to go out because we've used too much brandy. Another pause and we light the 'bomb', which blows out more streamers and whistles. The noise is terrific.

Clearing up is very easy. Black plastic sacks take away all the day's rubbish and washing-up is kept to a minimum. Too much effort is made to compete at Christmas. I don't give expensive presents because I can't afford to and anyway the measure of a gift is the thought and love behind it. I won't make myself a slave to Christmas because I know I would make everyone else miserable if I did.

I don't *believe* that Christmas is a time to salve my conscience and tolerate people I dislike – I can do that for the rest of the year. I feel women should try to put Christmas back in its place. If you have the time, and love making the dinner yourself, do so. But I'm a really lazy cook and so I like to do as little as possible and take short-cuts when I can. It doesn't matter because no one is there to criticise: we are all there to have fun and celebrate.

Christmas has become such a chore for most women that few honestly enjoy it. It has lost its true meaning of a child being born two thousand years ago who changed the world. All of us who have held our own children know that earth-shattering moment when 'unto us a child is born'. We must treasure Christmas as we treasure our children. Happy Christmas.

(Originally published December 1980, as 'How I learnt to enjoy Christmas', reprinted by kind permission of *Cosmopolitan* magazine)

GENTLE PARTINGS

Gentle partings was an attempt at trying to share the pain with lots of other people. I, who had counselled thousands of women and many men over the years, now turned to them for comfort. By now I felt as if *Cosmopolitan* readers were my friends. They shared their lives with me in letters, on the street and in trains. In return my articles reflected their feelings and my interpretations.

Some relationships end in a dramatic explosion. Some, like mine, wither quietly. Either way the pain and the grief is comparable to the death of a loved one. There is all the provision and conditioning for marriage and none at all for the breakdown of the most important relationship of one's life. Now, with more and more marriages ending in divorce, a third of the children will have to accept two sets of parents, and some several. It may be that unlike the concept of 'till death us do part' we will have to come to accept that life is now a series of transient ralationships, and when the end comes it must not be a horrible mutilating of two human beings who once loved each other, but a sensitive, caring separation of people who should try to remain friends.

When we decided to part after seventeen years of marriage, we faced the dilemmas of all couples having to become separate human beings, after sharing as one. The first agonised discussion was on his side. He faced moving out and living alone unable to bear the expense of keeping himself and the children and living any kind of dignified life of his own. Divorce puts an impossible financial restraint on a well-meaning man. Secondly, I retained the family home and the children, and he would suddenly become the stranger who visited his own home. We spent ages doing sums and trying to find a solution because we both argued that above all the hurt and pain that we might be feeling with each other, the children came first, and we owed it to them to part as gently as possible and owed it to our own sense of integrity to treat each other kindly.

The first idea was that he would build a small studio at the bottom of the garden but really ex-husbands, along with fairies, become a joke when discovered lurking on the fringes of one's life-style. Also we would have been unable to have any privacy from each other. We decided to build a studio at the top of the house, which would have been ideal, but proved as expensive as a deposit on Buckingham Palace. So finally the whole family sat with furrowed brow, until it became obvious that the basement of the house could become a flat and the children would all move up to the top two floors with me. Since they used to sleep in the basement, they would move into my bedroom, I would make half the sitting room my bedroom and all would be well.

We set a date – appropriately enough 5 November – for the 'upstairs downstairs' arrangement. Now it is quite one thing to make all these arrangements rationally and another to carry them out, without bursts of anger and sorrow. I don't pretend that it was an easy time. In fact, because we chose to share the house during the time we were making the arrangements and converting the flat, it all had a dream-like quality about it. As far as the children were concerned, they expressed their own hurt and anger with both of us very directly. I think it is only people who have been through the process of separating and destroying that very necessary unit for the survival of children, who can truly understand the anguish of a child. We spent time together talking it over with the children and by our-selves, and the value of the proximity of the two of us meant that all emotions could be dealt with immediately. The children were given the security of the fact that their father was not abandoning them. He would be there for at least two years, the time it would take to get a divorce.

The reality of beginning to experience us as two separate people, both of whom were united in one love for them, was apparent. So they did not have to suffer, like so many children, either a parent leaving or a move which left them disorientated and uprooted from their familiar surroundings.

We always had a party on 5 November. Our children and their friends looked forward to their father blowing himself up in great style in the back garden while I provided baked potatoes and beer, with my fingers in my ears. Indeed several of his friends would join him banning the children from touching the fireworks because it was too dangerous, and each producing a more horrendous explosion than the last. Even though it was our day of parting, the children decided that they still needed the reassurance of family routine, so it went ahead. I got in the food and he went to Hamleys and returned with the fireworks. Guests arrived and were ushered into the sitting room. For several days a carpenter had been making a partition across the sitting room. These things take longer than expected and he hadn't finished, so there he was hammering away with all my clothes and bedding very visible through the gaps in the boards. The friends who arrived were unaware of any separation, so there ensued a very Pinterish evening with the carpenter sawing and crashing away in the background while the guests made no reference at all to the fact that something unusual was going on – and neither did we. Looking back, I am amazed at our inability to say anything and then later on to find how threatening the breakdown of our relationship was to our friends.

That evening I went to bed in my own bedroom. I woke up the next morning feeling a mixture of dread and elation. I had never had a room of my own in my life. Like so many women, I lived at home, shared dormitories and then flats, and then married. However, neither had I ever really had total responsibility for myself, and the prospect was terrifying. Every so often I would feel an uncomfortable sense of panic, as though the world would come crashing down around me. I also felt a strange sense of physical amputation, an enormous sense of personal loss of what had been half of myself. My greatest consolation at the time was Chiswick Women's Aid, where the mothers I used to comfort now comforted me.

At first we laid our ground rules for not invading each other's privacy. To begin with we guarded them jealously. If he came upstairs to talk to me and so much as opened a cupboard, I would become unnecessarily angry. On the other hand I would cheat and send the children down to get anything I had run out of. He is organised, and he always had extra light bulbs and lavatory paper. I am forever sitting in the dark tearing up bits of the *Guardian*. Gradually, we regained our sense of humour and found we could laugh at ourselves.

Most of the humour was needed in dealing with other people. Some of our friends thought it was positively indecent not to scratch each other's eyes out and have a good fight. When it came to my first invitation to a man to have dinner with me, it was a disaster. I had explained the family setting, but he sat nervously at the edge of his chair with his eyes riveted on my husband, who was cleaning up the garden. Matters were not improved by my son, who charged through the room shouting 'adulterer' every twenty minutes. I never saw the man again, but my son began a campaign which raged upstairs and downstairs to terrorise any man or woman who came to the house. Two years later, he is much calmer and more able to let us make friends without feeling threatened. But I had a struggle for a while making it perfectly clear that I was his mother and he was my son, not my custodial guardian. It took a long time of being secure and stable for him to realise that any relationship I will make in the future will be serious.

One of the most important decisions we made was to stay out of the hands of lawyers. We should have family courts, where the law is there only to record the fact that the marriage has broken down. Until we do, we will have little chance of gentle partings. The whole legal system is based on opposition – forcing people to do battle. Credit must be given to the President of the Family Division, Sir George Baker, who had the vision and imagination to see that it need not be a legalised bun fight.

We decided to do a postal divorce. My husband had to fill in all my forms as I am incapable of seeing one without feeling a violent urge to tear it up. Even then, one of us had to apply to divorce the other – it would have been nicer if there could have been no blame.

The day of the hearing was horrible. In a postal divorce, you need not attend unless you have children, and then you must

79

satisfy the judge concerning their welfare. We had decided that as we owned two houses I would have them both, pay the mortgage off, move to the country on the proceeds of our present house and put the rent from the other towards our living expenses. This way he could keep his salary, only being responsible for clothes and holidays for the children. I would supplement my needs with writing and lecturing. Both of us were happy with this arrangement and we set off to see the judge.

The High Court in the Strand is designed to terrify people. Fortunately, I know lots of people who work there as I am often there with my mothers. You see the judge 'in chambers', i.e. in an informal little room, if you can call anything informal in a court. By definition, you feel a criminal. We had to hold hands by the time our turn arrived, we were both so nervous. The judge was kind, but the clerk had not expected my about-to-be-ex-husband to turn up as we were supposed to be enemies. We were directed to a long table, and the clerk did his best to isolate him up one end, but we very firmly sat close together – restraining a need to clutch each other in pure fright in case the judge mistook our motives. The judge asked me about the family and the children, and I gave my usual lucid explanation, which gave him a headache, so he asked me to go into the little witness-box and clutch the Bible, which I did. It is difficult for people to comprehend the relationship of two natural children, two grandchildren, four other assorted children, three dogs and two cats. However, we struggled through and then it was all over.

We left the court and went home and drank a bottle of champagne. In spite of the tensions, I believe accepting a 'no-blame' situation and parting without destroying each other is essential.

However one analyses a relationship, it always takes both people to make it and both to destroy it. Maybe in the next decade we will come to accept that the law is really irrelevant in determining human relationships and has no business here.

I feel most passionately that if and when matrimonial matters (or is it matrimonial affairs?) end up in court, then every effort must be made to make the experience comprehensible and bearable for the principal actors: the man, the woman and their children; not for the solicitors, barristers and judges. Whether the divorce and/or custody is contested or not, a legal system must be created that treats each family as a special case.

What I have in mind, and the idea is not new, is a family court where, in a sense, the interests of the family come before the strict procedures of the law. I would like to see a situation where the judge sits the husband wife down and says, 'You two shouldn't really be here because this is unavoidably a court of law and relationships have nothing to do with the law. But since you both find yourselves here as a matter of last resort, and certain things have to be sorted out, then we shall settle this matter in a way that is most sensible, least painful and that the both of you can understand to be just.'

I was speaking to an American friend about divorce, courts, custody and other like things that drive us to distraction, and he outlined for me some of the methods used in the United States: 'For a start we have the concept of "no-fault divorce" where neither party is cited as the "guilty" one. However, the Family Courts come in where there is friction between the parties or when there is some other problem of settlement. The workings of these courts vary from state to state, but basically everybody sits down informally (that is, around a table in a comfortable room, with no gowns, wigs or "my lords"), and the judge decides on the settlement and custody after hearing from everybody concerned. He or she has wide powers and is less bound by traditional court rules. For example, the judge will sit and talk with the man, the woman and their kids, and any welfare officers; they don't necessarily have to give sworn evidence or be formally cross-examined by other lawyers. Or take the instance when custody of the children is contested and one parent claims the other unfit; in this case the court is empowered to investigate these claims fully. The welfare of the children is the most important principle, and the court can override other legal protections of the parents in order to protect the kids.

'Although it's still a court of law and makes binding decisions, this system organises itself around the fact that where relationships are concerned, people are emotional and irrational. The Family Court is an attempt to accommodate legally a unique area of human life.'

Divorces are a painful and sometimes nasty business. What I'm asking for, pleading for, is that all of us approach them with some of the good feelings that we had when we entered the relationship. And along with that, we must all demand a legal system which recognises this and deals with the breakdown of marriage with some humanity.

(Originally published October 1979, as 'Divorce – keep it gentle', reprinted by kind permission of *Cosmopolitan* magazine)

THE ANCHOR – SUMMER 1965

This poem captures some of the enduring, happy memories of that marriage. We used to take our daughter and our friends to a pub called The Anchor in the summer of '65. I think this is the first poem I ever wrote. It belongs in this sequence of events because, though it was a very painful time for the whole family, it made me conscious that there were very good things in our marriage that should not be obscured by the bitterness that is inevitable in a divorce.

Sunday by the lapping river
deep welling mud lipping the high concrete walls
covered in crumpled shrimp shells.
Pint upon pint in militant rows stand before us.
Small boys with long arms leap from old boats
and weave in and out of the latticed cranes.

Soon it is November, the long wall is deserted,
rain sweeps the cobbles.
The children have gone, the beer is too cold.
We drink wine in Dr Johnson's room,
hearing him snort indignantly at the idle
Sunday chatter.

THE MOURNERS

1965. An attempt to fictionalise what actually happened to me when my mother died.

The telephone rang in the hall. He looked across at her. 'You answer it.'

The silence between them had lasted for at least half an hour. She hadn't eaten, she sat watching the familiar distasteful sight of her father shovelling food into his mouth.

'We shouldn't have left, it's probably the hospital.'

'Why don't you answer it and find out?' he said.

The telephone receiver was warm from the September sunlight lying in broad bands across the wide hall. The light picked up the silken colours of the Shanghai carpet and caught the pointed spikes of an African blow-fish gathering dust above the drawing-room door.

'We were just making her comfy,' said the slightly aggrieved voice of the Matron humming over the wires, 'She slipped away . . . Blessing really,' she said as an afterthought.

'Yes, I suppose so. My father and I will drive over as soon as he's finished eating.'

The shriek of his knife against a plate found a hollow pain inside her. She put the receiver down and looked at the protruding eyes of the blow-fish. The dust dancing along the sunlight confused her into believing that the left eye closed for a moment in a blowsy wink.

'Who was it?' he shouted.

'It was the hospital to say she died ten minutes ago.'

Standing a few feet away she was amused to see him cross himself. First time in thirty years at least, she thought.

His eyes flickered over her, registering at once that any theatricals would be wasted. The plate under his heavy face congealed slowly with white hummocks of potato protruding from sloppy gravy.

'I'll get the car – be ready in five minutes.' She turned on her heel, leaving him isolated and imprisoned in the gentle, gracious dining room.

Driving precisely along the narrow Devon lanes, listening to his piteous monologue, she found that third gear became a soprano duet with the grumbling bass of his voice as the car climbed. They pulled up in front of the french windows that had been her room. Inquisitive patients shuffled past watching them slyly – terminal cases, she thought clinically.

Her father strode forward to Matron standing traditionally in the doorway. 'In your hour of grief . . .' she heard the Matron say, releasing big fat tears down his cheeks. Gusty sobs tore his chest as he was led indoors, leaving her standing on the gravel path. Her hand brushed a large rose-bush. Her fingers curled round one of the blooms and slowly crushed the head. Passing her hand across her face, she could smell the familiar dry-sweet scent. It intoxicated her for a few moments and she closed her eyes. She heard the grating of the french windows opening on to the gravel, and through her lashes saw him standing framed between them.

'Come and kiss your mother,' he commanded.

She obediently followed him into the room. It was unchanged; the same flowers and the bowl of yesterday's apples glowing dull red in the dim light. Only the figure on the bed was different. No longer whispering and crying, she lay still, looking faintly disdainful. The girl bent and kissed the cheek, surprised at the unfamiliar coldness, and then walked out of the cool room into the sunlight, waiting patiently for her father to join her.

He cried all the way home. The news had spread and the neighbours gathered. In small clumps they came to call. Her father told and retold the story. 'For the best,' they said. 'Merciful release.' Relations arrived in flapping black shawls and black-armbanded suits – big, voluble, Irish.

'Look at you,' her father said at one point. 'No tears all day.'

She knew she was blushing; he had a large crumb at the

corner of his mouth. Does he know how ridiculous he looks, she wondered.

Much later it was dark and the relations left. She closed the door on the last of them and turned to go upstairs.

'I'm going to bed. Goodnight,' she said.

'I shan't sleep,' he called to her as she was halfway up. 'How am I going to live without her?' he bellowed.

'You'll manage,' she said dryly.

Upstairs she paused outside her mother's bedroom. Looking through the door she could see the clothes hanging quietly in the cupboard, and small shoes, size four and a half double-A, lying in neat rows. The pain in her chest frightened her. Outside the window the moon glistened on the river. Standing quietly she could hear the house moving round her, settling for the night. Opening a drawer on the dressing table she came across a glove lying on its back, still spread to the shape of her mother's hand, and she smiled gently to herself.

From downstairs came a rumbling snore. On the sewing table under the window she found the handbag brought back with her mother's personal effects. It contained five pounds, which she put in her pocket.

It took half an hour to pack her clothes. Before she left she looked in at her father sleeping soundly with his head thrown back. A log crashed in the fireplace and cinders flew. He opened his eyes, and they stared at each other for a moment before he grunted and rolled his head away. She left by the side door, down the path to the station. The train drew in and she chose a non-smoking carriage. Halfway there the ticket inspector passed by and was disturbed by the large fair girl pressed into the corner of the carriage with tears running down her cheeks.

'In love, I expect,' he thought sympathetically, and envied her the extravagance of her emotion.

86

THE FORTRESS

Before our separation, I had begun to write my second book *Infernal Child*. Looking at the previous unpublished short story, written in 1965, you can see how much I needed to write that book. What precipitated my writing an autobiography, when really I was too young to claim any right to bore people with my life story, was the result of a television interview.

I had just finished making a film with a director who was a personal friend of mine. We were finishing an hour-long interview and I was tired and vulnerable. When he asked me about my childhood I regressed back to those unspoken years. When I finished speaking I was in emotional agony. I, who for years, had regressed women and children back to their primary pain and betrayal to heal them, had been regressed myself; but there was no one to put me back together again. I wrote this account of what it felt like to both the director and the cameraman, to warn them to be careful in the future. But even that was not enough to stem the pain, so I wrote a book about it. By the end I was whole again.

She had a fortress round her soul behind which crouched a frightened child. The child built that fortress to protect itself from the unimaginable pain of not being loved. Each time its mother pushed it away, another brick was added and the pain was kept away from the child. Each time the father raged, the walls grew thicker and over thirty-seven years it had become impenetrable.

An interviewer with a cameraman crouched beside him filmed the woman sitting on the floor recording her explanation of her work, and stealthily built a bridge of empathy and trust across the floor to the door of the fortress.

'Do you want to talk about *your* childhood?' the interviewer said gently and the child, unused to brilliant interviewing techniques, broke through the door and spoke. Years rolled away, and the child told the voice how bad it had been. She recalled the fear and the pain, and then she stopped. The voice said 'cut', the camera stopped. The crew got on with the job of dismantling the equipment. The bridge disappeared, and when the child turned back to the door it had slammed shut. The child was alone, with no defence from the pain.

It will take another thirty-seven years to build a fortress. What will the child do now?

PRAYING

I was asked to do a television interview in Ulster. I was terrified because I'd never been there. I took Mike Dunne, a colleague at the Refuge, with me.

We were both horrified when we took a taxi to our hotel. The taxi driver decided that it was his duty to show us the streets where lurked instant death. I suppose I was fairly immune to war, because so much of my young life was spent in war-torn countries. I was only three when my family were captured by the Japanese and we were exchanged for high ranking prisoners-of-war.

'Michael,' I said, 'you're very quiet.'

'Well,' he said, 'I've always been taught that if the butter-flies in your stomach are flying in formation, you're all right – mine aren't.'

At this point, a huge green helicopter seemed to be chasing us down the road. 'My sweat glands have packed up,' said Mike.

The city of Belfast looked like a set of rotten teeth. The soldiers running up and down the streets looked pathetically young. The smell of violence hung over the city, and the people went about their business as usual.

We did the show, and the next morning I went over to the 'Peace House', which had been set up by the two women who started the Northern Ireland Peace Movement. Mariead was one of them, and both of us were feeling a little bit desolate. We talked for several hours, mostly about our very strong religious beliefs. When I got home I felt so grateful to her that I decided to write her this sort of poem. I don't usually do that, but I always enjoy it when I get poems from complete strangers who don't want anything from me, not even an acknowledge-ment – they just want to share a feeling with me.

In my alone place is an empty chamber
an internal room that is bare
the square is perfect and the whiteness
holds the harmony

Some days the harmony is disrupted
my inner self and quiet space can feel
frenzied until I sit quiet and reflect
my life is a blink away from death
and harmony returns

I need the joy of my inner world
so intensely that I have to accept
the alone – I have never found anyone
who can respect the need for such an individual space
that they will allow me my relationship with myself

I need to be loved without possession
I need to give love in abundance
as free flowing as milk to anyone who needs it
I have realised that my most joyful moments have
often been with a chance acquaintance who has made
    a remark
that has widened my perception. I catch a glimpse of the
    infinite

I wish I could distract myself day to day
If I do I feel real anguish
I need my alone even if I cry with loneliness
It is hard to bear
Mairead said she would pray for me
that was comforting knowing someone believing in the sam
but different harmony is also in a quiet space – praying

RUNNING ROUND THE BEND

I think women are always haunted by the fear of going mad. In a very male world – with everything geared to structure, facts and figures – a hazy, intuitive, gut instinct attitude to life is very threatening to men. I've often been described as mad by some and downright dangerous by others. So, as I skated nearer and nearer to the edge of a breakdown, Charing Cross Hospital became my refuge. I was very lucky because I had good friends to care for me during those long, dark months. My twin sister was like a rock, and my good friend Pat Wright would sit for hours by my bed while I babbled incoherently.

Like so many women, I had spent far too many years trying to cope with other people's problems, so that I had totally ignored my own needs. Indeed, I was really a walking, roving resource centre, allowing everyone access to myself and my time. Also, most damaging of all, I allowed people to criticise me, to undermine by self-worth, and above all, to question my integrity. It took a lot of skilled work from a caring psychologist called Bill Mitchell to make me come to terms with the fact that being constantly available to service other people's demands might well suit a missionary or a nun, but in spite of a convent upbringing I had all the guilt but none of the vocation. Therefore, I was on a vicious merry-go-round of servicing my feelings of guilt by meeting other people's needs, and then feeling resentful.

At that time of my life I was just finishing a major part of my own personal research into the roots of violence. Women's Aid, as I had known it, was changing into Family Rescue with a board of management, and in my heart of hearts I knew it was time for me to leave. Although I loved the mothers and children, I was surrounded by parasites of one sort or another.

But gradually Bill helped me to shake them loose. The poem *Nightmare* (on page 99) explains what it felt like.

I had a bigger response to this article than to anything I have ever written. To all those who wrote to me I replied with the refrain: breaking down is only a prelude to rebuilding; learn to do it with courage, because it should be your salvation.

I am writing about what is loosely called 'having a nervous breakdown' because I am so amazed by the reactions of people who hear me talk about it. Recently I was doing a book promotion tour for *Infernal Child* and I was repeatedly asked by journalists how I coped with the strain of running Chiswick Family Rescue. 'I didn't,' I said, 'I've just had a nervous breakdown' – stunned silence followed by embarrassed shuffling of feet then, 'Oh dear, I am sorry.' Women particularly come up to me in the street and say, 'How brave of you to admit you had a breakdown.' The final outrage was a woman who knows me slightly saying, 'Be careful of Mrs Pizzey, she is unstable – she's had a nervous breakdown!' At this point I would like to say that having a 'nervous breakdown' was the best thing that ever happened to me.

I have read and understand the political arguments that explain why people break down. I truly believe that most mental hospitals do more damage than good. Mental ill health in this country is at best a social problem which is continually ignored as the medical profession buries its head in the sand and continues to dish out pills, E.C.T. (electric shocks) and injections to deal with the symptoms of ill health instead of dealing with the root causes which are ninety per cent due to malfunctioning within the personality.

I do feel that the Women's Movement is right in its analysis that women and men are conditioned into their roles in life very early on. By about two years old, a little girl knows as she watches her mother that she will grow up to rear children. Even if she does no more than bear kids, she has fulfilled herself and society by giving birth. The temptation is that we can fall into the trap of just being a baby machine attached to a man.

For a man it is harder. From being tiny he has to make his

own destiny – not for him the biological reassurance of immortality. All he has is the expectations of his parents. The mother usually expects academic excellence and the father physical excellence. Either way for him he loses contact with feelings and emotions, while the girl is expected to lose contact with anything other than her loosely defined 'femininity'. That means she can achieve anything she likes till she marries, and then she is outlawed by society for at least five years per child while she does the most valuable work available to the human species, i.e. bringing up the next generation of children. Unfortunately it is easy for the rage and despair that accompanies the ostracism of a mother to pour over into her relation with her partner. He, usually bemusedly, feels guilty but also angry because he works all of God's hours to maintain the trap. In between them grow the fractured children.

Women break down and fill mental hospitals more than men partly because it is more socially acceptable for a woman to have a breakdown. She can be written off as neurotic or unstable, but a man risks losing his job and his perception of himself as a strong male. As everyone knows, anyone with a womb is bound to be emotionally suspect, and admitting to a breakdown is largely seen as a female occupation, whereas a man breaking down is seen as behaving like a woman.

The interesting thing about breaking down is that it is really a process of disintegration of the psyche. I came to a time in my life when I really needed to let go of all the strains and tensions of years of refuge work, a broken marriage, an adolescent son, grandchildren, money worries – the list is endless and not very different from anyone else's. I disintegrated volcanically and tried the patience of doctors and nurses, until I finally came to terms with the fact that I needed to rethink my self and then make myself whole again. It was a daunting prospect. I discovered to my surprise that I had avoided life's pain by cutting myself off from my feelings. I felt passionately on other people's behalf, but when I felt hurt and tension I blocked it off. The only measure of how I ached would be raised blood-pressure.

I would never have known that I had raised blood-pressure if I hadn't dropped in at a local family-planning clinic to see if they would change the pill. As a routine they took my blood-pressure and let out loud screams and ran around in circles. I assured them that the sight of rows and rows of dutch caps leering at me was quite enough to give anyone blood-pressure, let alone make them sterile for life. However, I had just changed to a very sympathetic doctor, who confirmed that it was far too high and suggested I go for hospital tests.

One of the major indications that you are going round the bend is that you think everyone else is. No way was I going anywhere near those awful places filled with malevolent white coats. Looking back, I am amazed at how patient my doctor was. I was awful. I missed appointments, felt sorry for myself, refused to do anything healthy like cutting down on drinking and generally crashed around my life surviving – especially last year – or on the brink of not surviving. The children suffered, because I became so tense that every minor irritant was a monumental disaster.

It is an important sign, I think, of disintegration when the major calamities pass by unnoticed but a minor one like my son's clothes in the hall produces a sense of murderous rage, followed by guilt and confusion. I spent weekends locked away in my bedroom just reading and sleeping. Finally I became so exhausted that I passed out. My doctor had had enough and said I would have to go to hospital. Fortunately I had heard of a very unusual man, who didn't believe in pills as a long-term treatment but looked at you as a person in your own setting and life-style – and then showed you how to get back on to the road of good health.

But before the long journey you had to let go. This was simply a matter of going to sleep for three weeks or whatever his team thought was the appropriate time. I was admitted to hospital clutching my teddy-bear and a library, escorted by a member of staff from Chiswick who plonked herself down on a chair and refused to leave me until I was at least starting to go to sleep. Tina's motives, though kind, were ulterior – the staff and mothers at the refuge were running a book on how long I'd stay in. Various nurses flitted in and out. A nurse tried to take my temperature. I knew I didn't have a temperature and I didn't feel like having it taken. She left quickly. Several other people left hurriedly and I felt furious. Soon the pills arrived and I obediently swallowed them.

I suppose I imagined that I would be wafted into a drug-induced torpor to wake up to a bright shiny new world. I'm afraid it's not like that. Letting go is difficult if you are essentially a fighter and have spent years not letting go. So it took weeks of ever-increasing pills, including Largactil, to get me to sleep. I discharged myself so often that the receptionists got quite used to a procession of anxious, caring people filing out clutching more and more of my equipment, while I charged the doors in my dressing-gown with my ancient teddy-bear as support.

Gradually over the weeks I began to talk to one or two of the doctors, particularly the houseman who spent hours listening to me rambling on in a pilled state about my fears and doubts. His patience through those long dark nights was amazing. So was the patience of all the staff. I began to come together when I finally comprehended that my blood-pressure was my own responsibility. I could see it shoot up if I became upset and go down if I was content. I reorganised a lot of my life. I realised that I am essentially a chaotic person who looks for order in other people, and I had to find some order within myself. I bought a diary and I was given a clock! I was on my way.

Two remarks made me feel good about myself having had a breakdown. One was a friend called Bridget, who said, 'You must have been quite healthy to let yourself break down,' and that I realise is true. I see many people now who should let go but don't dare for fear of what might happen. The answer is not to be afraid, because at the end of the tunnel is a greater understanding of yourself and therefore others around you. The other friend laughed heartily when I told her about my breakdown, and said she'd had a simply fabulous breakdown herself, because she thought she was God and spent weeks reorganising the world and her colleagues at work, who were much too embarrassed to hustle her off to a hospital.

I left hospital just before Christmas. I am free to go back if I need to or just to see the team as a friend. I know they are there, but I am pleased that I am slowly being able to deal with myself.

It did take a while for the Largactil to leave my system. I remember trying to write and my pen wandering across the page so I couldn't form letters. I still can't drive long distances;

and I get 'bad days' when I feel confused, but I know that those are the days to stay at home and relax. It's given me a much better perspective of myself and of my relationships to others. I no longer let people invade my space. I am much less frantic about living at full gallop. I have been taking a great interest in gardening, and to my surprise I can grow flowers. I have made a change from being tossed by circumstances into being in control of my own circumstances. I look back with great affection at the time I was in hospital and the time I spent recovering.

A woman in the Refuge last week said dramatically, 'I have just had a nervous breakdown.' There was a pause while we all looked at her. 'So have I,' I said. 'Wasn't it wonderful!' We both laughed. I hope in time to come a breakdown will not be seen as something sinister but as a prelude to growth, like winter before spring. It isn't whether you have a breakdown or not. It is a question of how you use it. For most people on the ward with me it was time well spent. Congratulations, class of '79.

I have always had a special fondness for people who are supposed to be mad. Very often after I have been on television or in the newspapers I have been visited by women who urgently want to speak to me. I always remember the first time I really sat down in the corner of a crowded sitting room listening to a little grey wisp of a woman telling me how she had been in a mental hospital. 'They gave me electric in my head,' she said. Then she explained she had glass all shattered inside her head. She described how whenever things went wrong for her she could hear the glass cracking and the splinters tearing and jagged in her skull. It was absolutely real to her. After several hours she finished telling me of her unloved, lonely and unhappy childhood, which led to an awful marriage and a dead child. It made perfectly good sense that her head was full of glass. I reassured her that as far as I was concerned I didn't think she was mad. I thought that it was her way of feeling pain and anguish, whereas others would feel different symptoms – like depression or repeated suicidal acts – or perhaps physically, with stress symptoms like ulcers. She smiled at me and we hugged each other. I don't think I did much for her, except that she left feeling that the whole world wasn't colluding against her and that we certainly all believed in her sanity.

Another much more bizarre situation occurred when I was in our tiny office with several mothers and staff. All of a sudden a furious, stocky little figure erupted through the door clutching a carrier bag to her chest. 'I saw you on the telly,' she said. 'Now you've got to help me.' Whereupon she produced two jam jars full of a yellow substance.

'What's that,' I asked nervously, in case it was what I thought it was.

'Fresh sick,' she said triumphantly. Top of the class, Pizzey, I said to myself, and tried to look helpful. 'It's poisoned – the fucker poisons me all the time. Every time I eat he slips it in. I'm ever so ill.' Roughly précis-ed for those with delicate ears and stomachs.

She had been fighting with her old man for years. She loved to hate him and he felt the same about her. He didn't beat her, but verbally tormented her until she became paranoid – to the despair of the doctor and the hospital, because nothing cured her of arriving clutching her bottles of fresh sick, demanding that they were analysed for poison.

Of course she was always told that there was no poison, and she would charge off elsewhere clutching her bottles. I think her local MP had a vintage collection. Her husband was also the despair of the local doctor and hospital, because he'd arrive every so often dripping blood where she had taken to him with whatever kitchen utensil was at hand. For someone who spent so much time sicking up she looked as if she could pack a good wallop.

Anyway, she put the two jars on the office table, pressed five pounds into my hand, said she'd be back next week to collect the samples and the report. I gravely considered the refrigerating properties of fresh sick. Then I considered how on earth I was going to deal with her, particularly as I had her money. So I sat down with a fair number of sympathetic mothers and we wrote a report for her on our official paper agreeing that in our opinion (and that of the committee) there were traces of illegal substances contained in the said jars. I chickened out of keeping the stuff in my fridge and bribed a willing adolescent to throw it out and return the jars.

When she came back the next week she was delighted with the report and actually sat down and had a perfectly sane, rational conversation about herself and her husband. It was a poisoned relationship, we agreed; but it wasn't in the sick, it was between them both. She laughed and said she loved him. I said I knew, and off she went happy as a clam. I don't know if she gave up the sick. If she did, I hope she didn't replace it with something worse.

(Originally published September 1980, as 'What my nervous breakdown taught me about myself', reprinted by kind permission of *Cosmopolitan* magazine)

NIGHTMARE

I nearly went mad in 1969. My husband was always away, and I was alone with two small children. The doctor put me on masses of tranquillisers.

See myself a creature no larger than a man's thumb
covered in a loose layer of pink flesh.
Shuffling on elbows bat-like, slithering and scuffling into
   dark corners.

Two eyes that span the top of my head – huge iridescent
   blisters
High over head a thin silver wire.
Mostly I perch somewhere in the centre,
sometimes I fall, headfirst into the abyss,
where I am at this particular moment.

Right at the bottom of this chasm live monsters.
They lie in oily sludge waiting.
I feel them rearing to meet me.
Their great rough bodies roll and barrel mine.
The noise is terrible. In the far corner is a cave.
I know this cave well and escape monsters into its warm
   mouth.

I creep willingly into the hollow webby darkness and lie
   waiting.
Dimensions of fear cease to amaze me.
At its highest pitch I hang suspended over jagged rocks and
   then
disappear deep into the earth,
a body spread thinly into the crevasses.

I lie in the cave, soft furry legs explore me.
I am preserved.

Eventually I move and find my left hand.
I gaze at the delicate 'U' bend between my fingers.
It gives me courage and I stake out my limbs and
feel liquid smooth flowing in my veins.

The flow becomes violent and I am ejected.
Out of the cave, through the monsters that roar and snatch,
back up onto the wire that hums and sings to me.

I hang upside down and wait.
Please don't disturb me.

REFLECTIONS ON BEING FORTY

This piece wasn't published for ages after I wrote it. I suppose part of the problem is that it was not at all fashionable in 1979 to celebrate your ageing process. I was born wanting to be forty. I could never understand all the veneration of youth. To me, it was an incredibly boring, dependent time on one's life. I woke up on the morning of my fortieth birthday full of glee, and the first thing I did was to pop over to the chemist and buy a bottle of Phyllosan, much advertised as 'fortifying the over-forties'. It seemed a ceremonial way of marking the great occasion.

Twenty-one was the landmark in my younger days. A wand could be waved and suddenly keys to the front door, greater responsibility and a euphoric future full of dark handsome men with ten thousand a year would materialise over the back fence. My mother had a carved chest full of satin and lace which had been ear-marked for the great occasion of my twenty-first birthday. Somehow this was to tie in with a coming-out ball and being presented to the Queen. The idea of being twenty-one seemed ominous in the extreme. As fate would have it (and fate is blessed with a marvellous sense of irony), instead of my coming-out and being presented, followed by a twenty-first party, my mother died. The Queen decided to abdicate from the responsibility of shaking hands with rows of acned daughters of the rich, and the teenage revolution got rid of the idea that twenty-one was where it was all at. I breathed a sigh of relief, reached the age of twenty-one and, like so many of my contemporaries, found myself pregnant, married and full of dreams of years of domestic bliss, surrounded by the patter of tiny feet – with a vision of myself rocking in my chair at the age of forty, white-haired and placid. At twenty-one anyone over thirty is old; anyone over forty is senile.

Now I am celebrating my fortieth birthday. After the twenty-one hurdle, forty was always the next. 'Fair, fat and forty,' they say, gives you gall-stones. Now I'm all three: fair thanks to Alison, my hairdresser; fat because I choose to be; and no gall-stones because I don't believe in guilt, which gives you symptoms. Every time a journalist asks me coyly about my age I am amused, because I am much happier at forty than I ever was at twenty or thirty.

At twenty I worried about everything. Was I a good mother/ housewife/lover/cook/bottle-washer/nurse/Christian/slave, etc? The answer was no to the whole lot. I was guilt-ridden most of the time, except for a few moments every New Year's Eve when I promised myself, God, family and relatives that I would do better. The euphoria lasted at least twenty-four hours before I returned to the gin, cigarettes, being rude to Aunt Bertha and yelling at the kids.

When I was first married we were broke a lot of the time. I had to put my daughter with a child-minder while I went out to work. I never understood how the world functioned; the necessity of the nine-to-five day, everyone arriving at the same time and leaving en masse regardless of the volume of work involved, made no sense. The need to dress like other people was also a nightmare. If I got a dress without a split or tear, even if I had to staple the hem up with the office stapler, I could never get from A to B without my tights laddering. The 'little office dress' looked ridiculous on my unshapely form. Some unkind employer remarked that I looked more like a candidate for the rugger field than a showpiece for his posh office. My reply had me sacked in two minutes. But I minded in those days. I cared what people thought. I tried to wear fashionable shoes that pinched my feet and creased my brow and ruined my temper. I cooked delicious meals à deux for my husband, and fed God knows how many friends and lay-abouts in an effort to be a good hostess. I sat through endless dinner parties listening to other people's plans for extensions to their houses and to holiday plans. I went on holidays with the family. Part of me enjoyed watching the children swimming and soaking up the sun; but much of me was dying slowly because those years were devoted to other people with no space for myself.

It was not just marriage and children, it was far more fundamental than that. Women then as now are taught to live vicariously, first alongside their mothers to serve in the family and then they are taught that their only real identity is through a man. Even though attitudes have changed dramatically in the last ten years and women have been cajoled and directed to look further afield and to consider careers and an independent life-style – scratch most women and you will find a three-piece suite. I wasn't any different from the others, but the break-up of my marriage brought me face to face with myself; the last two years of my thirties have made me look at both what I feel I have achieved and where I feel I have failed.

Women are so much luckier than men. We can give birth, and that fact alone gives us a sense of immortality. Once a girl goes into labour and then holds the baby in her arms she is catapulted from the confines of her own ego boundaries into sharing with another. This experience unites all women. Even modern technology has not destroyed it. Men, who have to create rituals only to have them destroyed, are far more alienated from themselves and fearful of the continuing power of women. To have children means desperate, tired, grey years of sleepless nights and constant worry, interspersed with moments of glorious pleasure. An early marriage, particularly with children, means that neither partner has had time to discover him or herself. The danger is that during the child-bearing years the woman lags behind, begrudging and boring, while the man forges ahead in his career and social life. Suddenly the children are all at school and the woman stands, like I did, in the hall of her house and for the first time hears the ringing silences and realises that she is biologically redundant – her children still need her but can survive without her. What is left very often in the relationship with her husband is the shared experience of the television screen. Some couples pull through this time and find new ways of relating. Some don't. Their paths are too separate.

In our case we decided to part amicably and with great care for the children. So while I consider the break-up of my marriage a failure, I console myself with the fact that we have managed for two years to share the same house and the children and have remained friends. We have completed a postal divorce without resorting to solicitors. The children, after a lot of pain, have accepted our new relationship; they can see the time we spend together or with the whole family as good times, distinctly better than the days when we would argue over our life-styles.

At forty I can look back and say with a real sigh of relief that I'm unmarriageable, anyway, so I won't do it again – but I don't regret trying. I fail horribly when it comes to being liberated in the more rigorous sense of the word. I still like perfume and I can't mend anything. Any machine blows up at the mere sight of my face, and I'd rather confront a violent husband than a blocked loo. I love plants but have black thumbs. I talk to them, even beg them to grow. I put them on the pill for a while because I read somewhere that hormones make them grow. They did flourish, but then overnight they drooped all over the floor. I didn't feel able to return to the contraceptive clinic and explain that I wanted a change of pill, so I gave up. My daughter now tends them and they flourish, as does anything she looks after.

I suppose the biggest sense of failure for any woman is when her children behave in such a way that they offend the mores of society. Certainly when I realised that my daughter was pregnant at fifteen I was shaken to the core. However, it was one of those events that start as a tragedy and turn out to be a triumph, for us at least. I don't advocate having babies at that age, but it just so happens that my grandson is the most rewarding pleasure of my life, and my daughter is a much better mother than I ever was. To have all the good times of a child's life and very little of the strain is my idea of heaven. When life is hard and the struggle is lonely I go to him, and his huge brown eyes snap with laughter and excitement and I recapture all the pleasures of my own children's exploration of the world around them. I know that now I am forty I shall probably see my grandchildren's children, and I feel very privileged.

What I feel I have achieved first of all is that I have actually survived to forty. Quite a few of my friends have died of cancer, and I have such awful vices like too much smoking, drinking and eating – much to my doctor's disgust. I'm amazed that I wake up every morning and feel strong enough to reach for my beta-bloka for high blood-pressure. Certainly I feel that there is now refuge for women all over England and in various other countries, thanks to the fact that Hounslow decided to prosecute me and keep the whole issue alive for so many years.

I also find that it is quite possible to make good relationships with men, once they realise that I want nothing of them except themselves. Because I have children, I have my own house and an income, be it ever so precarious; my need for male relationships is purely for the pleasure of male companionship. I now have many men who are my friends, but I don't expect them to be like my woman friends. I don't think men are at all like women, so I don't want to domesticate them. I like the difference. Working with men whose minds operate completely differently to mine is very creative and fulfilling. I also value my relationships with women. They are long-lasting and deep.

So I am forty now and able to enter calmer waters, having understood some of my own needs and those of others.

The fears of old age are always there. I don't have a full-length mirror, which is just as well. I dread the moment when the tops of my thighs look like an elephant's behind. I console myself with the fact that elephants have to live with it – indeed they look quite cheerful – but I don't look forward to it. I suppose it's always easier for someone, like myself, who has always been outsize to accept the ravages of old age much more gracefully than women who have traded on their bodies. I have just acquired a pair of glasses because I decided touring three or four times round a roundabout in the car in order to read the signposts was a waste of valuable time. The effect was electric. Suddenly everything took on an awful clarity. I always thought the misty haze that I floated through was the after-effects of alcohol but no, it was short-sightedness. However, I prefer the misty blur, so I only wear them at roundabouts.

Looming over my head is the subject of menopause. Everything conspires to make women aware of the dreadful time when, according to the media, the medical profession and other women, you are no longer 'a woman'. Somehow once you no longer menstruate you are relegated to the back corridors of life, sexless and boring. I have never understood this attitude at all. Why shouldn't women decide that the menopause is nature's way of giving us a whole new lease of life without having to worry about contraception and childbirth? In fact, it should be a time when sex can be exclusively for pleasure every day of the month if you feel like it, instead of that confusing mixture of biology, bleeding, lust and affection. There is always an uncertain feeling at forty that if you are going to have another child you need to make that decision now. It is strange to think that there will be years when you will not be able to consider pregnancy and another baby, but it is illogical. I accept now that the milky smell of a new-born baby triggers off a broody feeling that makes me hover round the window of a shop selling baby clothes. The remedy is to send my daughter out with my son-out-of-law (how else do I describe him?) and spend the night with my rampaging grandson. I also have this secret vision of myself behaving very badly, being drunk and disorderly, knocking off policemen's hats, shop-lifting bars of chocolate and telling to astounded magistrates it is all because of my hot flushes. Well, if 'The Hulk' can get away with it, why can't I?

I'm glad I'm forty. I wouldn't like to be twenty or thirty again. I think lots of women would agree with me when I say that even if society tries to make you feel old and ugly because it reveres youth, the pleasure of finding yourself and the confidence in knowing much more about yourself far outweighs the magazine images that remind you of the passing years.

The next time I shall be this reflective is when I am eighty years on. I shall write another piece from a raft floating down the Amazon with a bottle of gin in one hand and a double-barrelled shotgun in the other. Growing old is just a state of mind – don't let anyone tell you any different. Happy Birthday.

(Originally published in Cosmopolitan's Guide to Looking Great 1980/81, as 'Facing up to Forty', reprinted by kind permission of *Cosmopolitan* magazine)

WHAT'S WRONG WITH CHASTITY?

I have to admit that there was a measure of duplicity about this article as I had been making notes and planning to write a venomous piece about randy men for ages, and I was halfway through when Jeff came into my life. I decided to write the piece anyway, but for all those readers who know me so well the end gives it all away.

As soon as I was officially divorced, I found myself being asked by friends if I had a man in my life. It might take one sentence or sometimes it would take all evening, but eventually it would come out, particularly after a few bottles of wine. 'Ah . . . um . . . well, have you got anyone at the moment?' Or, 'I bet you're having a good time.' Single women were more direct: 'Sleeping with anyone?' Married women tended to be a bit wistful: 'Lucky you – all those men.' (Then, pulling themselves together hastily), 'Not that I don't adore Nigel/Crispin/Rupert . . . wouldn't change him for the world.'

Newspapers asked boldly, usually in the middle of the night or at the crack of dawn when, even if you did have a man in your bed, it would be enough to make him impotent forever, hearing himself discussed with a strange voice from the *Evening Slaughter*.

The reporter would start in a bullying tone, 'Mrs Pizzey – it is Mrs Pizzey, isn't it? – not changed to Ms? . . . Ah, I see Women's Lib not your style . . . I see, you *are* Women's Lib but don't think that's a very relevant issue . . . I see . . . Still at the same address? . . . I see. How's hubby these days? . . . Oh good. Still good friends? . . . I see . . . Has he got anyone? . . . I see . . . Of course, of course I'll ask him myself . . . Now, while we're still on the subject, I've been told there's a new man in your life? . . . Lots of new – oh really?' (Sound of drooling and rapid breathing.) 'Wait a minute. Could you say that again? . . . Oh, I see.' At this point, I would say very patiently that I had lots of men in my life who were my friends, whom I loved dearly. Many of them had wives whom I also loved dearly. But no, there was no man I was romantically attached to.

'Romantically attached to' is the euphemism used by the media instead of talking about sex. It is always worth being polite to gossip columnists, I discovered to my cost, because 'no comment' gives them a licence to print what they want. Usually at this point in the story, the gossip writer would lose interest.

I would find myself sleepless with outrage. It wasn't outrage at the question itself, because I like a good piece of gossip as much as anyone else. I'm the first person to read a gossip column or to ring a girlfriend to hear who's doing what unto whom. It was the attitude that if you didn't have a man in your life (or, more explicitly, in your bed) then you were somehow a failure. You were someone to be pitied and sighed over. Perhaps you needed a new deodorant? Change your perfume? Have a face transplant? To be manless is considered an un-natural state of being for a woman, whereas if a man is without a permanent girlfriend, he is considered to be a randy bachelor.

I was very defensive at first. I would react with savage sarcasm if asked about men. I would point out that after seventeen years of marriage, one deserved a parole for at least several years from a one-to-one relationship. One thing I learned, after watching other people's divorces, was not to leap straight out of one relationship and into another. Time and time again, I saw people I loved rush out and make a choice out of pain and loneliness. I knew it was imperative to be on my own. I remember the pain of the loneliness in the early days. I remember the ache of the absence of affection from a partner, and also the sudden knowledge that I was free to sexually enjoy a relationship with someone else.

I learned to deal with the sudden surges of lust by laughing at myself. I accepted that I was a normal, healthy woman, and thank God I still felt randy, and please God, don't let it rust. I arrived at a state of chastity through a conscious decision after several abortive attempts at complying with society's demands that everything happens in twos, like ears, eyes, feet, etc. Society's demands appeared most strikingly in the attitudes of men I encountered.

A typical example of men's attitudes to a lone female arose when I was asked to dinner by a very nice couple. Lucy knew me well enough to mention the fact that it was all couples and that she had kindly decided to lumber me with a bachelor friend of theirs whom she had been trying to pair off for years. I arrived in a mini-cab because I knew that I drink more than the legal driving limit, and anyway I can't tell my right from my left when I'm sober, and after a glass of wine I can't decide which side of the road I'm on. I was introduced to three couples, each of which sat huddled together. All the women had neat hair-does and imitation Cartier shoes. The men had pinkish faces and wore old school ties. The conversation wittered on and on about rowing eights and the City. The women talked about their au pairs' sex lives in lieu of their own. The bachelor sat next to me. 'Oh God,' I thought, 'he is one of those who is convinced I'm desperate for it.'

He was one of those hopeless Peter Pans, a bit thin on top and thick around the waist. I knew he was a jogger and kept an exercise bicycle in his bedroom. His hands were flabby and well manicured. I probably made him nervous, because his handshake was slightly wet. When under stress, I resort to large gins, so I was sinking them down as fast as possible till it was time to go to dinner where, of course, I was placed next to him.

By this time he was getting more and more attentive. He kept asking me about my ex-husband, my family, and eventually got round to the subject of the new men in my life. 'I don't have any – and I don't intend to,' I said very firmly. He moved his thigh up against mine and got all moist around the lips.

'Don't you miss . . . er . . . um . . . s— well, it?' he said gazing despairingly at the couples who were well into next year's holidays.

I decided not to beat around the bush (so to speak). 'Yes,' I answered. 'Very much. But there is nothing wrong with choosing to remain celibate until you find someone you really love, and if you don't, maybe remain celibate forever.'

He looked completely startled. All his life, he had played bed-hopping with women. It never crossed his mind that a woman could gain a good enough self-image not to have to service his needs in order to prop up her desolate feelings about herself. 'I say,' he said, probably deciding that my problem was that I hated men, 'you are a very strong woman.'

'Not at all. I just like myself. That's all.'

He couldn't quite give up, though. He insisted on driving me home instead of letting me get a mini-cab. When we got to the door, before he switched off the engine, I said very primly, 'Good night, and thank you.'

'No coffee?' he said.

'No coffee. And I don't want to go to bed with you ever.'

'Let me know if you change your mind,' he said. 'Women in your condition do get a bit peculiar.' I slammed my door with such fury that it shook the foundations and I cried myself to sleep.

Married men were even worse. I never knew how many of my friends' husbands played around until I got divorced. Dick was an absolute pain, particularly as he knew the children and could drop by as a friendly adopted uncle.

'Dick,' I would say, 'why don't you go home to your wife?'

'Must see you and the kids are all right,' he would say, lurking around me like a huge German shepherd.

He ate like one, too. He always arrived around mealtimes and then he'd gaze soulfully at me over his pile of potatoes.

'I really worry about you, you know,' he would say shovelling a huge mound of food into his mouth. 'What's a good woman like you doing without a man? It's your life – it's not natural. And I've been meaning to tell you for ages . . .' (leans over the table with a sincere caring look in his eyes) '. . . it's making you bad-tempered.'

'Dick,' I'd reply, '*you* are making me bad tempered . . . I am worried about your wife, who is home waiting for you with dinner burning in the oven. Go home.'

Usually his leaving the house was a battle: lots of cheerful goodbyes to the children, followed by an undignified two-step as I tried to stop him kissing me on the mouth.

Dick was one of the 'never-say-die' school of men. At least he was not malicious. The men that really could leave gaping holes in my growing sense of self were usually very insecure in themselves, and any attempt at refusing an advance was seen as a personal rejection. I was chatting with a man at a party and was genuinely enjoying our discussion when it was time for me to leave. He asked if he could take me out to dinner. I didn't like him enough to spend a whole evening with him, so I gracefully explained that I needed an early night because I'd had a heavy day at the Refuge. His charm dissolved immediately. 'What you need,' he said, spitting out his words, 'is a good screw.' Why I thought to myself as I went home, do so many men think that all a woman needs in her life is a man's prick?

I talked all this over with Priscilla. Priscilla fills me with admiration. Unlike me, who struggles hopelessly with life, she sails along on a tide of narcissism that allows her to lead a particularly charmed life. God has been good to her. She is beautiful. In fact, she is so in love with herself that she has no time to bother with men. She has a theory that as long as she never allows a man to make love to her, she remains fatally attractive to all men. I must say there does seem to be some truth in this theory. She always makes sure that they all meet each other and vie with each other to keep her in the style she fancies. One man is her gas bill, another the electricity, another the rates, and the only favour she bestows is a chaste kiss and a warm smile at the most expensive restaurant she can find.

Priscilla is chaste by design. She says she'll never find a man who can satisfy her as well as she can satisfy herself – a thought that rather shook me, but I imagine that a look in the mirror is all it would take for her. Still, I do find her such a solace, because she has a lovely sense of humour about herself. When I'm feeling insecure, I know she is nearby and is probably hustling another Asprey diamond off some lustful male.

Polly is quite different. She's our local rent-a-body. She says she is a totally liberated woman and that she can define her own sexuality, which she does with boring regularity over endless bowls of lentil soup. I used to get very taken in by her descriptions of wild nights with a series of men who passed through her bed with a time-table that would be the envy of British Rail. Most of the time, she seemed to be happy, because (she explained) 'orgasm is the ultimate high.' So it didn't seem to matter who was at the other end, as long as she achieved her highs. When times were lean, she confided that a massage machine was her standby. I have never been able to look at them in shop windows without blushing.

It did, however, become obvious that a lot of the talking was a desperate attempt to convince herself that the procession was more than just a way of keeping her from spending time with herself. Indeed, the very thought of a night on her own would drive her out into the streets and into anyone's house that she could invade with any excuse. I don't think she will ever change. I can see her growing older and more desperate. She diets. She buys her ethnic clothes from the best junk shops. She wears Earth Shoes and exudes a damp sexuality, but it never seems to turn out right for her even if she is always joining causes and championing the preservation of fungus in Ulan Bator.

Everyone else has lots to say on the subject of chastity. I looked with awe at Mother Teresa and women like her who throw themselves into a totally giving way of life with seemingly radiant confidence. I discovered the pleasures of living alone and slowly appreciated the peace of a bed of my own. I don't think I could ever share a bedroom again. Waking up when I want to, reading at five in the morning, allowing my books and papers to crowd the floor, letting the piles become dusty mountains, drinking endless cups of coffee followed by endless trips to the loo without worrying about waking anyone, staying for hours in the bathroom reading the back of all the labels, never having to share the Sunday papers, cooking when I feel like it – and then not at all for days, burying myself in growing herbs when I have always believed I had black thumbs – these are all pleasures that I found within myself. I was directing so much of my partnership energy into doing things I had never done before, like going camping on my Greek island. The only things that shared my tent were a rat and a huge spider. I philosophised that a four-legged rat was a better bet than a two-legged rat, and he behaved very well, keeping his own space behind my suitcase.

I think women have a real choice which many ignore. Liberation doesn't mean you have to succumb to the pressures of feeling that to be a woman you have to behave like the worst stereotype of a randy man. You do have a choice, and if there is a period of time, maybe many years, when there is no relationship that is emotionally fulfilling, well, it's no disaster. Chastity is not a derogatory word for me; it merely means I like myself enough not to feel ashamed to be on my own. I'm sure there are many women who feel the same.

Jeff, who read this article, said: 'What about men with horny women chasing them all over the place?' Yes . . . Men too have their problems. Maybe they should have their say. He's gone off to think about it.

(Originally published October 1980, as 'Why don't men understand about celibacy?', reprinted by kind permission of *Cosmopolitan* magazine)

FEMINISM AND THE FAMILY

I felt that Betty Friedan had put her finger so accurately on the pulse of all women all over the world who desperately wanted to have good warm loving relationships with men, that it was important not just for me to go and hear her speak, but also to follow it up with an article for *Cosmopolitan*. I knew the audience, both male and female would respond positively, and hopefully there would be a much greater attempt for men and women to communicate with each other. Certainly, I was pleased with the letters I got.

Betty Friedan, the high priestess of the American Women's Movement, came to London in late 1980. I read her book *The Feminine Mystique* ten years ago, and it literally changed my life. Now I had the chance to hear her speak in person. I was expecting the usual fiery rhetoric that one's ears have become accustomed to from the rantings and ravings of the lunatic fringe of the Women's Movement. *The Feminine Mystique* was an angry book. It broke through all the suburban barriers of the perfect woman at home, in the office, as a mother and a lover. It said that men were the exploiters and that the world was run by men especially to keep women chained to the kitchen sink, dependent and desperate. A lot of what she said was true, and millions of women rose up across the world and demanded their equal rights with men. This book was followed by a spate of other books, articles and magazines. Everywhere, small groups of women banded together to talk about women's liberation and the new freedom.

For me, ten years earlier, as a thirty-year-old-housewife and mother of two small children, participation in one such group was a traumatic experience. I remember my first women's liberation meeting with crystal precision. It was the first time in my ten years of marriage that I had gone out at night, leaving my husband behind to baby-sit. It had never before occurred to me that I should want to go out without him, but I had been fired by the idea that the isolation and loneliness I felt as a mother with toddlers could be shared with other women and that a solution could be found that would enable us to live happier and fuller lives. So I gritted my teeth, found the house where the meeting was held and knocked on the door.

It was a large Victorian house with steep stairs and dark corridors. I was led upstairs by a rather abrupt young girl, who looked at me as I stood nervously on the doorstep as if I smelled. I did smell of Femme eau-de-cologne; she smelled of BO. Lesson number one: smelling nice means you are oppressed by the perfume manufacturers (who are, of course, all men); smelling of sweat shows you don't use deodorant or perfume and, therefore, are a good member of the Women's Movement. You must ignore the fact that you are oppressing the rest of the human race if you inisist on inflicting your BO on everybody else. Once in the room, which was large and square, I saw two other women who looked like me. They wore dresses and make-up and looked as frightened and out of place as I did. The other eight could have come off an assembly line. The movement uniform consisted of jeans and jerseys and a lot of grubbiness around the edges. The two new women and myself sat on the sofa together and exchanged apprehensive glances. I was ready to cry. I had been reading about 'sister-hood' and love and sharing. Here there was only anger and hostility.

The three of us were asked why we had come. I said because I was lonely with my two small children and a husband whose job took him away a lot. I loved them all but felt I was a cabbage and I passionately believed that women could organise together so that we could share our lives while we were with the children. The other two said very much the same thing. Our words hung in the cold air of disapproval from the concentrated gaze of the group. Buck-toothed, bespectacled faces glared at us from all around the room. The group's leader, the 'convener' as she introduced herself – who had the biggest teeth and thickest wire-rimmed glasses – then launched into a long speech about our lives. It was full of incomprehensible words like 'polemics', 'dialectics' and 'categorical imperatives'. This was a foreign language to us, understood only by the select members of this exclusive club which we were, apparently, too inadequate to join. We were briskly told that our problem was not our loneliness and isolation, it was our husbands and they oppressed us. The lecture made us feel as if we had been naughty schoolgirls all our lives. We were told we had been making the wrong choices. What we had to do was to cast off our shackles, to rise and take up the fight alongside our sisters.

I was particularly told off because I confessed that my beloved Janet came twice a week to help me muck out the house because I was such a failure as a housewife. Teeth and glasses whinnied with the convener's rage. Not only was I a middle-class member of the parasitical bourgeoisie, but I was also directly oppressing another woman. 'But,' I said meekly, 'if she didn't work for me she'd have to work in a factory. And we like each other.' Teeth and glasses poured scorn on such reasoning. 'At least in the factory,' the convener said, 'she could join the rest of the working class and rise up together and overthrow the capitalists who are grinding the faces of the poor into the dirt.' It was all very strong stuff. We were all given a cup of coffee from Habitat mugs while Chairman Mao gazed benignly down upon us from the cork-tiled walls.

The three of us left together and exchanged addresses and said we would meet again, which we did. I went home to my husband, who said how lonely he had been while I was away. I gave him an earful on how he had oppressed me all our married life, and I spent the night sitting bolt upright in bed, working out a list of men who were personally responsible for my oppression, starting with God.

When the three of us got together again, we all agreed that we would return to the consciousness-raising group and try to explain to them without getting angry or emotional that we very much loved our husbands and our children, but what we wanted to do was to be part of a movement that would help women to use their childbearing years more fruitfully. We had chosen to have children and we wanted to be with them while they were young, but we didn't want our other talents to be ignored while we were at home. We wanted to meet all sorts of other women and to share our resources and to be part of our community. After all, it was women like ourselves who before the industrial revolution were the social workers, the midwives and the health visitors, and we were responsible to and for each other. It all seemed reasonable enough to us.

For the next meeting, I wore trousers and no make-up. Sal did the same. Phoebe, on the other hand, overreacted as usual and wore an outrageous skirt, wads of make-up and shoes that would give a foot-fetishist a heart attack. We didn't get anywhere with our explanation. There were more women there this time, all young, mostly unmarried and at universities. They laughed themselves silly at us. What we were hoping to achieve would hinder the coming of the revolution, they said. Society had to be destroyed and out of its ashes would emerge a wonderful new world. They were a bit vague as to exactly how this new world would work, but there was a general consensus in the room that there would be no men around. 'No men?' said Sal, who was as naïve as Christmas. 'What do we do for sex?' I stamped heavily on her foot and muttered, 'Tell you later.' I thought if Phoebe didn't pull her skirt down quickly, we would be likely to find out sooner.

The meeting finished with lots of resolutions about 'The Working Class', which was a bit odd as there were no representatives of the species in the room. It seemed rather hard on the women at the Brentford Biscuit Factory to have pickets on their behalf when no one had even asked them how they felt. But these women obviously had the revolution well in hand, and the likes of us weren't wanted, which is just as well because Phoebe got stuck into opening One o'clock Clubs for mums with kids under five, and I started Women's Aid, which turned into a refuge. Sal is still up to her eyes in kids and dogs, and her husband washes up but refuses to do anything else, and they love each other. So, ten years later, I now asked myself, What would Betty Friedan have to say to anyone like me?

I must say here that the account of my experiences in this particular group is subjective. It happened that way for me. There were thousands of groups meeting all over the country and many of them gave solace and comfort to many women. Unfortunately, England inherited the worst dogmas and dogmatists of the Women's Movement from America. The early days of the movement were dominated by strident, hostile American Women, many of whom had fled from America as a result of their revolutionary activities. They brought their particular brand of politics to this country, and cashed in on the growing awareness of themes that were central to women's lives. Contraception, the right to choose an abortion, and equal pay and opportunities were all issues that united everyone. Unfortunately, other demands crept in as well. Twenty-four-hour nurseries was one of the thorniest. Everyone agreed that if a woman had to work, then of course good child-care should be provided. But we didn't dare say that many of us would much prefer to stay home with our kids, because we would be made to feel stupid.

Many good things have come as a result of the ideals of the Women's Movement. Better conditions of work, non-discrimination and sexual equality are among the benefits. But, as I see it, the losses have been enormous. By far the greatest damage has been done by a handful of vocal, powerful women who have turned the Women's Movement into a religion of hating men. As a result, men have become hostile and suspicious of women instead of being encouraged to care and share with us. Many confused women catapulted themselves out of their marriages, taking the lonely stand as a single-parent family on the promise of a dream of sisterhood that would take away any need to work at a relationship, because men were just there to be used. Newspapers didn't help any, because they tended to print only the hysterical outpourings of fanatics, except for the writings of Jill Tweedie and Mary Stott, who held the centre, but not many women had access to their columns.

When I arrived at the American Embassy with Jeff to hear Betty speak, I assumed that Jeff would be the only man in the audience. I was pleasantly surprised to find several men there, and the majority of women present looked far more representative of fifty-two per cent of the population than the usual turn-out of the heavy-boot brigade. Betty Friedan herself was surprisingly small and delicate, although no less passionate. But what blew my mind was her message.

The Women's Movement, she said, had achieved great things in the last ten years, but now we had reached the second stage. In the beginning, we were all so busy fighting for public justice that feminists were guilty of ignoring what was central to all women's lives – the family. We in the audience all sat stunned. We were expecting the usual rhetoric, and here was Betty, sharing with us all what had been concerning most of us for years. She explained that we knew that women are naturally communal and caring. We also knew that we now had the freedom to choose whether or not we wanted to have children. But it was an inescapable fact that children need parenting by both men and women.

Here was a world-renowned figure, gracefully able to admit that she was at as much of a loss as we were as to how to even begin the dialogue between men and women on the future of family life in any country of the world. One thing was for sure: the family would always exist in one form or another. But it was a generally shared agreement that the nuclear family was a disaster, serving neither the parents nor the children. The absent father and the lonely isolated mother took their frustrations out on each other and on their children. For most men, the advent of children meant an albatross of debt for the rest of their lives. For the mother it meant years of exhaustion as she tried to be a cook, maid, laundress, child psychiatrist, pediatrician, teacher and chauffeur. Then she was told that she was 'only a housewife'. How did anyone sustain a warm loving relationship with those monumental pressures on their shoulders? They didn't. People were bailing out of marriage faster than we had parachutes, and more and more single-parent families were joining the bottom of the heap in our society. Betty didn't offer solutions. She is a wise woman and left us to think for ourselves.

I have no solutions, except for my own belief that it must be women who take the responsibility upon themselves to make it public that the role of bringing up children is the most important job in this or any country. No longer should we feel guilty and useless because we are housewives. The Women's Movement must represent the needs of women who joyfully choose to stay at home and bring up their children. No woman should be forced to go out to work against her will and leave her children because there is insufficient money in the family to provide the essentials of human life. Running a family should be seen as a profession in its own right. During these years, educational provisions should be made so that women who wish to re-enter the job market at a later stage can do so. This means you can go to college and take your children with you.

Jobs should be available for women in the community. They should be able to run and staff refuges, social services, health centres and any other caring agency you care to mention *with their children*. I have made it a policy for ten years that my Refuge should employ women with children, who are welcome to come with their mothers. I have run an international organisation with children on my knee as they pass in and out of the office. Why did we ever allow children to be excluded from real life for sixteen years, before they finish school? Why did we exclude ourselves? All these questions must be answered.

We need an International Year of the Family so that money is made available for men and women to get together in harmony to plan for a new future. We are lucky that Patrick Jenkin (then Secretary of State for Social Services) is dedicated to the concept of family care. We must move now before the resentment and hostility between the sexes make the concept of love and caring between a man and a woman merely a part of history. The chilling and sinister prophets of the Women's Movement who advocate hate do not speak for us all. That night in the US Embassy, Betty Friedan rekindled for me a faith in the future of the movement which preaches that all women are our sisters and surely now that all men are our brothers.

(Originally published May 1981, as 'Can you be free inside the family?', reprinted by kind permission of *Cosmopolitan* magazine)

THE 300 GROUP: IS THERE A WOMAN IN THE HOUSE?

This piece was written at the request of my editor at *Cosmopolitan*, Pat Garratt. It was sparked off by the re-emergence of an attempt to get more women in the House of Commons. I always feel guilty because I am one of those women who go on and on about getting more women into Parliament, but when I was once asked if I would stand, I fell about in heaps of laughter and said certainly not. When Lesley Abdela began the 300 Group in 1980 I saw it as an opportunity to assuage my conscience and write in support of her movement. Quite honestly, the only way I could ever see my role in Parliamentary affairs is as part of a demolition squad. I would like to see the historic buildings preserved, but a modern businesslike approach to governing this country.

Do you know that there are six hundred and seventeen men in the House of Commons, and only nineteen women? 'Why?' we all ask, every time this embarrassing fact comes up. The answer seems to me to be fairly simple. The House of Commons is run like an exclusive men's club, the members of which are not about to allow us women a chance to spoil their fun and games. Quite honestly, as I have parked my bum for hours on those uncomfortable gallery benches as the fate of battered wives is discussed by a bored and indifferent chamber, I felt that no mature adult could bear to put up with all the nursery nonsense that goes on there. I definitely feel the motherly need to smack Reggie's hand or to put Norman in the corner. The interesting thing is that all the men in the House are terrified by Mrs Thatcher's no-nonsense approach to real life. Whether you like her politics or not, you must admit that she does get on with the business of governing, which is a welcome change from the feet-on-the-table approach of the male leaders of yesteryear.

The 300 Group was born out of the passion and vision of Lesley Abdela. She is immensely enthusiastic, and has a sane, commonsense attitude towards encouraging women to stand and take at least half the responsibility for running the country. The 300 Group is propelled by a small, dedicated core of women who do not wish to divide men and women or to promote women at the expense of men. Rather, they seek to achieve equality between the sexes, hoping that by accomplishing this aim, the country will reflect a better balance.

Personally, I feel a little more militant than that. I am sure that if we had an equal number of men and women making decisions at the top, we would quickly remove all those dangerous nuclear missiles from the grasp of the male members of the House and return the warheads to their spoiled brats of friends in America. I would also imagine that an overnight improvement in the quality of life would replace the race towards an even higher level of technology that annihilates and disregards the human need people have for each other.

The 300 Group held their innaugural meeting in the House of Commons on Tuesday, 25 November, 1980. The room was packed with women and a few men. The atmosphere was electric. There was a glow on the faces round me that I hadn't seen since the early days of the Women's Movement.

You could see what a great loss it has been to Parliament and to the country that women have been subtly ostrasised by a structure that ignores their needs as women. At the moment, you cannot be a wife and a mother and a member of Parliament unless you can afford expensive help at home. Most successful male members have equally able wives. The divorce rate for MPs is high because the hours are impossible. As in all good clubs, most of the business is done on the nod or in the bar. The men certainly don't want this changed. Hours and hours are spent in tedious sessions, nit-picking over words with bossy civil servants. The debates in the House are a time for showing off, and the level of debate is embarrassingly low. Think of six-year-olds arguing over conkers, and it about sums it up. All of this needs changing so that a woman need not abandon her family if she wishes to stand for Parliament.

The special appeal of the 300 Group is that it is working for ordinary and capable women who are willing to stand for election. I certainly expect my readers to be among that number. The Group will offer a back-up and a training programme. They are hoping to, and indeed have already started to, set up support committees up and down the country so that women out of London will have equal opportunity to be involved.

Are you a capable woman? If you are, and you wish to stand or to support this Group, write to:

Lesley Abdela
The Mill House
Burford
Oxfordshire.

Send stamps, because, like most women's organisations, they have limited funds.

(Originally published February 1981, reprinted by kind permission of *Cosmopolitan* magazine)

OPINION PIECE

This piece was also written at Pat Garratt's request. It was never published because, I think, I was supposed to be militant about name-changing. But I think a lot of women feel as I do, so I've added it to this collection.

What's in a name? A lot of aggro, as far as I'm concerned. I was originally called Erin Carney in those far off days when I was a maiden. I didn't think much of that name, or of my father, come to think of it, and I couldn't wait to get the name changed. I had always envisioned having a romantic, Byronic surname – something like La Marquise de Verdi Boudiller. Pizzey was a bit of a come-down, even if it was originally De Puissie from northern France. The trouble was the pronunciation. One irate gentleman once wrote to me 'Pissey by name and Pissy by nature'. That put the whole problem in a nutshell. I have been called 'Erin Pinney' and, even more annoyingly, 'Mrs Erin Piggey'.

During my more militant days, I went through a period of believing that it was wrong for women, like slaves, to have no names of their own, so I would have to find a suitable name for myself. 'Why should you be forced to use the name of your captor – your oppressor? After all, women have a *herstory* of their own,' dictated the local radical feminist. I consulted my children. My daughter pointed out that if I called myself by any name other than Pizzey, everyone at school would think she was illegitimate. She had a point there.

Lots of my friends were experimenting with various prefixes, the most common of which was 'Ms' instead of 'Mrs'. It looked all right in print, but 'Ms' in conversation sounded like a distressed wasp.

My husband at the time was well known as 'Jack Pizzey' long before I became publicly known for my work at the Refuge. Eventually, I wrote books and articles under his name. We were a family with children, and both of us pursued our different careers. When we divorced, it didn't cross my mind to change my name. I think years of fighting over serious issues like refuge for all women and children took me away from the original niggling obsessions of the Women's Movement. But when I decided to re-marry, I was faced with the name-game all over again.

Oddly enough, I naturally assumed I would take Jeff's name and become 'Mrs Shapiro'. On a very practical level, why should I keep my ex-husband's name when I was no longer with him, but married to another man? Both the children would obviously keep their father's name, but there was no legitimate reason for me to clutter up the way for a future Mrs Pizzey. On an emotional level, Jeff and I promised, albeit in a registrar office, to be together forever. As far as we were concerned, we walked out of that office together as Shapiros.

Everyone else didn't see it quite the same way. Somehow, they argued, if I didn't remain Erin Pizzey, all those years of hard grind at the Refuge would be swept away at the change of a surname. 'You can't change your name,' said a journalist. 'Nobody will know who you are.' It seemed almost as though anything I said or wrote would be totally invalidated if I wrote as 'Erin Shapiro'. They assumed that the public would only choose to read something supplied by someone with 'a name'. I chose not to believe that.

There are a whole raft of insecure people who trade on their names. They are usually people who have done nothing to earn a name other than to have an accident of birth that gave them a title. They use it shamelessly, and are encouraged by the fawning, grovelling behaviour of the English class-ridden system. I have had many marvellous encounters with people who recognise me and who are a pleasure to talk with, like a man who quoted Wordsworth to us when I was introducing Jeff to Tintern Abbey in Gwent, and like a lady outside a Bristol pub who hailed me loudly through a crowd and said I'd rescued her from suicide with a *Cosmopolitan* article ('Fabulously Fat' – see page 64). The other side of the coin occurs at gatherings of a few people when I become the target for everyone's awful marital relationships. Any dinner with friends, and I'll be pinned in my chair by a distraught husband or wife while everyone else is into the gin.

At the end of the day, I have to admit that I'm incurably romantic. I like being Jeff's wife. That's the problem with women – we're a soppy lot. So here I am, for better or for worse, Mrs Erin Shapiro.

WHO SAYS YOU NEED
A BETTER HALF?

The problem with living on your own for a long time is that if
you are fairly solitary, like me, you get to like it. A lot of the
philosophy in this article is about other couples, but also
underneath it all I was having to decide whether I really
wanted to go back to sharing my bed, the bathroom, the
morning newsapers, the children and my life with a man again.
So traumatic was the decision that I had to extract a promise
from Jeff that he would retire to another bedroom should the
merest hint of claustrophobia assail me. As usual it is never the
major issues that prove to be the most difficult to resolve. No,
it was far more a question of who read the *Sunday Times*
supplement first.

When I was a child I was fascinated by the fairy story of the
princess and the frog. There the princess was bending over this
cold, slimy, warty animal when suddenly she felt compelled to
kiss it – ugh! However, so the story goes (thereby helping to
condition another generation of little girls) the frog magically
becomes a handsome prince and they live happily ever after.

I was a particularly nasty, suspicious child and after the little
girls had stopped sighing over the teacher who told this story, I
went to the frog pond to observe for myself. There were no
princesses, and no handsome princes – if you discounted the
school gardener. There were only frogs sitting on top of each
other like a double-decker sandwich – the bottom one looking
pretty miserable about it. Years later I rewrote the story for
myself. Actually, what happened is that she bent over and
kissed the frog and turned into a frog herself, whereupon he
jumped straight on to her back and she had to lug him around

for the rest of her life! If you don't believe me, have a look at a pair of frogs for yourself. There she is looking utterly weary and desperate while he sits there blinking contentedly – they look just like the couple next-door.

We have been brainwashed from infancy into believing that our salvation lies in the arms of someone else. The whole of civilisation moved from tribal life, in which there was a vast choice of relationships, to the extended family, in which, in Victorian times, it was not at all unusual for some members of the family to be bachelors or spinsters with a useful role in the family, to nowadays, when to be on your own and not part of a couple is considered positively dangerous and indecent. A person who remains on his or her own is indeed a threat to couples. Remaining on your own because you have chosen not to form a one-to-one relationship reminds a couple of the freedom they have denied themselves.

I have no objection to people living in pairs. My complaint is that the moment they do, they change. Take Jo, as an example. For years she would come round in between rows, abortions, relationships and scandals; we would talk the night away, awash with cheap plonk and good humour. Until she found The Man. From then on she changed. The dreaded Couples Syndrome had hit her. She would never come round without him. He would sit lumpily in the corner gazing at the fridge while she filled his glass and made him sandwiches to keep him going. No longer did she sprawl in a heap on the floor but perched on the edge of a sofa, lunging at him now and then to remind herself he was still there. On each visit she became more and more matronly, until I could bear it no longer. The last time she telephoned I said I wanted to know her as she was – the way I liked her. I felt it was an imposition that I should be forced into a relationship with her relationship. I haven't seen her since. Pity, there goes one of the last revolutionaries down the road to suburbia.

Then there are my lovely wild men friends who vow they will never marry. 'Who me!' they say knocking back the whisky at four in the morning. 'Never. Not the type.' They are right. Most men I know would make lousy husbands and should have warnings tattooed on their foreheads. However after a few weeks' absence you get to know the signals. 'I'd like you to meet Miranda/Jane/Charlotte,' said a slightly subdued voice at the end of the phone. 'OK, your place or mine?' 'Ours,' he says. That usually means that instead of our wild drunken night full of lunatic laughter, it's sherry, followed by avocados stuffed with blotting paper prawns, followed by a roast (he carves). Pudding is chocolate mousse; the wine is in wine glasses. The place is clean – so is the conversation.

I leave early because she is sending laser beams of hatred across the room at me. They are a couple – but, of course, being a man, it doesn't take long before he is back round at my place with her pinned neatly to the house with a child or two. 'Don't you think you should go home?' I say at about nine o'clock, just as he is on the point of getting stuck into my fridge. 'She doesn't mind – we have a wonderful relationship,' he says. 'I do my thing and she does hers.' Hers is babysitting and eating the remains of the burnt dinner which has been sitting in the oven for hours in return for the dubious pleasure of saying 'we' at the few social functions she will be able to attend.

There are people who marry or live together and get it right. People who genuinely have a marvellous, warm, equal relationship lasting longer than twenty minutes. There must be. I feel it's like fairies; if you believe in them hard enough, they will exist. I believe in this as much as I believe that children should be brought up by both parents, but it seems less and less successful.

With relationships blowing up like mines all around me I have come to the conclusion that before it is possible to have a good relationship with anyone else, it is necessary to have a relationship with oneself. That seems alarmingly obvious, but from an early age one is conditioned to think of oneself in relationship to a member of the opposite sex. If you don't get to be an angel at the school nativity play and get goosed by a shepherd, you're never going to make it. Because of my size and height I was always Joseph, which may explain my independent attitude.

Most couples I know have a sort of 'Polyfilla' relationship; it's like shoring up a crumbling wall. They meet and immediately fill each other with whopping lies. He says he wants a free relationship that is based on trust and affection;

which, translated, means she must be monogamous and stay at home cooking – while he is free to wander. She says she wants exactly the same thing as he does. Which, translated, means she wants him to marry her so she can settle down and have babies.

What usually happens is that they are busy propping up each other's lies and filling the gaping holes in the relationship with bunches of flowers and delicious casseroles until it slides into ultimatum time. She either gets pregnant, or says marry me or else I'll find another. (A. N. Other is always on the scene by this time.) He has then got to pack or give in. As a rule the longer they live together the less likely he is to marry. After two years most men have remodelled their partners into their mothers, so leaving is traumatic. The only value in all the misery of a lousy relationship is that it does make some people stop, think, live on their own for a while, and get to know that really warm, nice lovable person – themselves. When in doubt get over the arms race. Spend time with yourself and everyone will want to spend more time with you.

Other countries have a much better system. Take Greece, for example. In a Greek family I know, where I am godmother to one of the daughters, there is no question of playing couples at all. While they are courting the couple do spend ostentatious time together, largely to prove to the parents that they are not anywhere else making love. Once the marriage ceremony is over, life goes back to normal and the women live their lives with each other and the children, while the men hang around together making plans to change the world.

In that Greek house it is quite common for the married couples to sleep apart or together as the mood takes them and, although the women do all the washing, cooking and domestic work, it came as quite a shock to me to find relief in not having a man cluttering up the draining-board or organising my shopping. Most evenings, the women would sit on the terrace talking while the men went off drinking, and there would be no frantic hanging on. They all had a full sense of themselves, so a partner did not need to be a crutch. Maybe frantic coupling is a symptom of the fear of empty people who, to fill that yawning gap, cram someone into it.

Perhaps we are moving into a world where we no longer

need either to own or to belong to someone in order to be fulfilled, but will find a new manner of loving that allows us to remain separate. One of the most relevant and beautiful pieces of writing that has ever crossed my path sums up this possibility. Called *Letter to a Young Poet*, it was written in 1904 by the poet and visionary Rainer Maria Rilke and ever since I read it (and re-read it) I have been aware of how far ahead of its time it is. It takes the view that we should understand the huge insecurities that underlie the feelings of women who care for their young, and appreciate the loss that men suffer when they realise they can never achieve this kind of immortality – unless they happen to create something that outlasts their own deaths. He writes:

'The girl and the woman in their new, individual unfolding, will be only transient imitators of bad or good masculine behaviour, and repeaters of masculine professions. After the uncertainty of such transitions it will be seen that women have passed through the exuberance and vicissitudes of those (often ridiculous) disguises only in order to purify their most essential being from the distorting influences of the other sex. Surely women, in whom life tarries and dwells more immediately, fruitfully and confidently, must have become fundamentally more mature human beings than light man, whom the weight of nobody's fruit pulls down beneath the surface of life, who conceited and rash as he is, underrates what he thinks he loves. This humanity of woman brought forth in pain and degradation will come to light when she has shed the conventions of mere femininity in the alterations of her outward station, and the men who today do not feel it coming will be struck by it. One day . . . the woman will be here whose name will no longer signify merely the opposite of masculinity, but something in itself, something which makes us think of no complement or limitation, but only of life and existence: the feminine human being.'

The first part of this letter very much describes the position many single women find themselves in when they are suddenly thrust into a world run by men, for men. Not that I am saying that men necessarily want it that way! I know plenty of men who hate the whole rat race as much as I do. But I also know the bewildering feeling of picking yourself up after a disastrous breakdown and wondering just what sort of a woman you are going to be if, most of your life, you have been thinking only in terms of darning the socks of your lover or, worse still, have spent years and years being a housewife. No wonder some women today go marching round with ties round their necks and large hobnailed boots.

As much as it offends me to see women acting out a male role that is boorish and offensive in the extreme, I do understand the very deep anger in many women, the very deep hatred women feel for members of the opposite sex until they can (and, thank God, most women do) come through that awful painful time and remember that they were told lies on both sides. It wasn't only that Daddy was the first prince, but behind him and sometimes far more powerfully there was Mummy whispering that she was entitled to think of herself as a princess. How many little girls go to fancy dress parties dressed exactly in that image? Or, even worse, go as fairies waving wands and never put the wand down for the rest of their lives – not even in bed.

However, I am now going to get back to the end of Rilke's letter, because I think it is the most important part, and a blueprint for relationships between men and women.

'This step forward will (very much against the wishes of out-stripped man to begin with) change the love experience that now is full of error, alter it fundamentally, refashion it into a relationship meant to be between one human being and another, no longer between man and wife. And this more human love (which will consummate itself infinitely thoughtfully and gently, and well and clearly in binding and loosing) will be something like that which we are preparing with struggle and toil, the love which consists in the mutual guarding, bordering and saluting of two solitudes.'

It is precisely the respect and caring without possessing that struck me most about that passage. Why are we not able as men and women to share what time we have together as special without feeling that some other part of ourselves is possessed somewhere else by someone else? It is this possessiveness that creates such destructive guilts. Most human beings are capable of loving many people: there should be nothing threatening in that.

So if a particularly sad-eyed frog blinks gently at you and asks to be taken on your pillow and then kissed, please remember what I have said. Nobody needs frogs except flies.

(Originally published December 1979,
reprinted by kind permission of *Cosmopolitan* magazine)

CAREER WOMAN OR
EARTH MOTHER?

I suppose I could have called this article 'The Empty Womb Syndrome'. I had received so many letters from women who either couldn't have children, or had left it all too late. I tried to write down all that I felt about the subject. It also reflected a decision I had made with Jeff. Because I already had two children and grandchildren I honestly didn't want to have any more. However, I realised that this meant that Jeff would have no children of his own. We are happy with our decision, and I wanted women without children to look at themselves positively.

'Barren' and 'sterile' are two words that haunted me as a child. I used to lie in the bath when I was about twelve, looking at my stomach, wondering if I'd end up like Miss Sykes at the post office. Miss Sykes had a moustache, big boots and no children – not even an illegitimate one hastily given away, like the one Maisie had, just to prove she could give birth – nothing except a raddled, smelly Jack Russell dog with a rude behind. I grew up with images not only of Miss Sykes but also of my huge, uncouth Irish aunts, three of whom had no children at all. 'Why?' I inquired of my mother. My mother never answered questions about subjects that could be considered remotely rude. Bearing children came into that category, so she merely looked vague and fearful, and attributed it to God.

Aunt Nita, one of the Irish aunts, wanted to be something in films. Her house was full of mournful pictures of her punting, wearing a huge straw hat that shaded her yearning eyes. She had those long white arms so admired in the Twenties. She once lifted her jersey to show me the bandages that kept her breasts flat as a pancake. 'You'll never find a man,' she sniffed, looking at my protruding chest. 'Times have changed,' I said, thinking to myself that all those bandages must also have restricted her ability to conceive. At the time, I had a very hazy idea of how it was done anyway.

The lady next-door to Aunt Mary had nine children. She was always passing by with a huge belly, a child on her hip and one in the pram. The rest of the children would scamper after her. Aunt Mary would suck in her mouth and mutter, 'Disgusting . . . Shouldn't be allowed.' I felt sure it was jealousy, though I never heard her bemoan her fate or express a desire for children. Her husband died after twenty-five years of marriage, so they'd had plenty of time to do whatever it was that they were supposed to do, but she was obviously 'barren' – that awful word that sounded as though one's inner world resembled something approaching a lunar landscape.

Aunt Florie was large and tough. She looked as if she might take umbrage if a shadow dared fall on her spotless doorstep. Her house was agonisingly clean. Her attitude to children was uncompromising: she hated them. Children were to be kept out of sight. When I was forced to visit her house I felt she would have preferred it if I had been relegated to the scullery. I never knew who her husband was. I gathered that he, too, was dead. I always felt his death must have been a merciful release. She probably buried him with a tin of shoe polish to make good use of his time. She was, according to the rest of the family, sterile. Sterile, I felt, was a harsh word suited to a woman like Aunt Florie.

I was brought up, like so many people, to believe that women were divided into two categories. There were those who could have children and were, therefore, automatically mothers (after all, that is what women were there for), and those women who couldn't have children and could never be mothers. These unfortunates were destined to remain incomplete people for ever. Of course, no one said anything as rude as that out loud; it was better left unsaid.

Looking over my shoulder at those childhood memories, they seem like the sepia photographs stuck in old family albums. I got married and had children and still assumed that there were only those two sorts of women.

Jean was a friend from my early twenties. She and I both giggled about the same things. We shared much of our lives together and she married shortly after I did. I was pregnant and she was not, but it really didn't matter at first. She explained that she and her husband wanted to wait anyway.

My daughter was five when I saw a temperature chart in Jean's bedroom. She was getting desperate. I was pregnant again. 'Wave a pair of trousers at me . . .' I said, falling about laughing. The look on her face stopped me. 'Do you know how bloody insulting it is to have you making jokes like that? Do you know what it's like, going to clinics and having strange men staring up your vagina? Blowing air through your tubes? Making you feel biologically redundant?' By this time she was incoherent.

She was in the grip of a huge technology that had been invented to make it possible for the infertile man or woman to have a child – something unheard of in my aunt's day. Listening to her, I wondered at the price she was having to pay. For her, making love over the last two years had been dictated by a rise in temperature. Such an artificial demand made the idea of a relaxed sex-life out of the question. She saw herself and her husband, Larry, as two automatic robots geared by the hospital team into bouncing on top of one another so many times a month. Then came the big moment when her period was a day overdue. Two days and they would dare hope, and then the awful let-down. The sympathy from everyone followed, and then she had to start all over again. She used to pretend that she had conceived on several occasions, but 'lost it', just to prove to herself that she could, at least, conceive. But in her heart of hearts, she knew she had never conceived.

She looked at Larry over those months with ever-increasing dislike, and her infertility didn't help his image of her. After all, as his mother kept pointing out, they'd never had any of that sort of trouble in their family. 'Those thin, fashionable women don't have child-bearing hips anyway,' the mother would say, adding that Jean's job was against the whole idea of motherhood. 'All that office life. Gadding about in those high heels. Food in packages.' Jean looked at Larry and thought, 'How can you fancy a man who has to wank into a test-tube?'

Larry looked at Jean and thought of the latest specialist's report that said that Jean's vaginal mucus killed his sperm. Jean finished talking to me, put down her coffee cup, and said, 'We're getting a divorce.'

Jean was distraught for such a long time after the divorce that I felt she'd never pull through. For all the beautiful, smiling pictures of women who held their miracle babies in their arms, there was an army of women like Jean, destroyed by the fact that they would not bear children. In Jean's case, she had to accept not only the divorce but also the knowledge that her ex-husband had a new wife with a little girl. She had to fight fierce feelings that somehow that little girl was, through Larry, part of her.

I listened when I could, between running a house and tending a husband. My children loved her as a favourite friend, but I felt twinges of embarrassment when she clung to the baby too closely or asked to have my daughter for a holiday. We drew apart because I was at home all day, encrusted in baked beans and fish fingers. I was an expert on whooping-cough injections and pre-school playgroups. She didn't know one end of a nappy from the other, and wanted to talk about her reports on staff management. I couldn't follow the complexities of computer software and the whole subject made me feel useless. Our friendship finally fell apart on my son's fourth birthday.

By this time, Jean had come to terms with being childless. It was odd for me, because all those years when I was giving birth and being a housewife, I had envied her her extra money, her glamour and her access to the outside world. Still I always felt a sneaking feeling of power, because even though I was a boring cabbage, I at least had children. Even if I did nothing else with my life except make superb rice pudding and wash whiter than white, I could go to my grave knowing that I left behind me a walking pool of genes, some of which would bear a slight resemblance to me – immortality, I think they call it. But, I would say to myself, fiercely gazing at my tear-stained face in the mirror after a particularly awful day with my husband and my children, even if Jean gets to be the managing director, she can only leave her name at the end of the annual report, and what's that got to do with immortality? 'What indeed!' I'd say, flaring my nostrils and returning to the kitchen sink to tackle the dirty knickers and the snotty handkerchiefs.

Jean arrived on the day of the birthday party just as ten malevolent midgets were dive-bombing the tea-table. She stood in the doorway and exuded elegance. I knew and appreciated the fact that she'd made the effort to get off work at four o'clock on a Thursday afternoon, but there was no way I could feel civil after I'd just produced a huge meal and coped with all those children. Seeing my son throw his arms round her, his face lit up with pleasure was simply too much. To add insult to injury, she had bought him an amazing clever toy that came from America and was unobtainable in England. We stood facing each other, feeling worlds apart.

She would always want to share other women's children because she had none of her own, and I was unable to allow her to share in my world. I had to pay such a price for having children, in a society that isolated and devalued me, that I in turn avenged myself on Jean for her freedom. It took years for us to come together again as friends.

Fortunately, though painfully, I learned that childbearing was not my only destiny. Now, Jean and I can look back, and we regret many of the feelings we experienced during those years. Jean regrets most of all the lack of counselling by the medical world that saw her only as a reproduction machine. Then, when she found she couldn't reproduce, she was abandoned and written off as an annoying malfunction and a tearful nuisance. Jean, however, was fortunate in that she was able to make the most of herself. She filled her life with a career that she loved and with many good and worthwhile friendships. She is aware that many childless women grow bitter and resentful in these days, when the extended family has disappeared and the surrogate roles that used to be filled by childless women are no longer there. But she has adopted several families and developed her resources in areas other than child-rearing, and come to feel contented.

Alison is quite different from Jean. I first met Alison about five years ago when someone told me she would come to my house to do my hair, saving me the awful trek to the hairdresser. Alison, it turned out, has a very definite outlook on childbearing (and, in fact, on everything). 'Barren' or 'sterile were not words one could use to describe Alison. She is tall, blonde and glamorous. She is very warm and funny. She seems to have an amazingly hectic social life and no ambition at all to get married. She had been married once, she said, but only for a few days. No, she had no wish to have children. No, not even the slightest twinge. In fact, she rarely liked children. There were the few exceptions, but on the whole she couldn't see what all the fuss was about. They just smelt of sick, as far as she was concerned. Dogs were infinitely preferable.

As a self-employed hairdresser, she travels all over the world. She works hard when she feels like it, and not at all when she doesn't. 'But, Alison,' I used to say, aghast at her attitude, 'what happens when you're too old for all that gadding around?'

Five years later, I am convinced that Alison will never be too old. She grew up in a healthier atmosphere than I did. She was never told her destiny was to marry and multiply.

She has lots of friends, many of whom are her own age (early thirties) and are career women whose relationship is to their own lifestyles. Sometimes they marry and have children, but they always remain true to their vision of themselves, whatever their situation. Theirs is an outlook that depends on their own definition of their place in this world. They are not ruled by biology, by society, or by the way other people see them. Married or not, with children or not, fertile or not, these women honestly respect themselves and their achievements. They do not submerge themselves in the expectations of others. I am very grateful to those women because they taught me so much.

Women today really do have a choice. Thousands of women have children only because they feel they ought to. If women truly followed the dictates of their own hearts, many would tell you they would honestly prefer a career. Unfortunately, many men agree to have children due to the same coercion. They succumb to society's pressure, which insists that there is something selfish about the idea of two people living together, uninterrupted by the patter of tiny feet. Certainly there are women who are saddened by the fact that they can't have children, but now with foster-care replacing children's homes, women who wish to mother can fulfil themselves more easily.

More organisations must be founded in this country to put childless women in touch with other children and families who could authentically benefit from their love. When I was lecturing in America, I came across an excellent organisation called Brothers and Sisters Inc. The 'brothers and sisters' were men and women who had no children but who adopted families where there was a shortage of relations. We could certainly use programmes like that here.

The words 'barren' and 'sterile' could well become obsolete if women who do not have children find that their lives are so full and interesting that those words are inappropriate. I have remarried and do not want children. We have made a choice. Biology is not our destiny – thank God.

(Originally published July 1981,
reprinted by kind permission of *Cosmopolitan* magazine)

MAN'S BEST FRIEND

I have always found it easy to befriend men. I grew up in a very male environment and I was 'one of the boys' until I was at least fourteen. As much as I enjoyed the company of men, I was always saddened by the suspicion I met on the part of men I tried to befriend. In fact, it usually took a very straight talk, when I made it absolutely clear that I had no intention of sleeping with him, before a man relaxed and we could enjoy each other's company.

I realised when I was five that I was a failure as a woman. Johnnie Nash was my best friend and he asked my sister to marry him – it still hurts. I said he could go ahead, because I was going to ask my mother to marry me anyway. She wasn't very interested in the idea – that still hurts, too. All my life I have been seen as a threat by most men, partly because I have always been big, but also because I have always been incapable of playing the war game between men and women. It's no fun being neutral territory like Switzerland if all you get is chocolate and cuckoo-clocks when you're looking for love.

The problem seems to be that men are horribly frightened by women. That is why a man's best friend is said to be a dog. I first discovered that men were terrified of us when I was fourteen. James was the toughest boy in our gang. Everyone admired him. He asked me to go for a walk with him after dinner. We walked and walked and walked. He said nothing; I jabbered like a parrot on LSD. He suddenly grabbed my hand, and I then realised he was terrified of me. His hand was wringing wet and shaking. Hoping to find something he would respond to, and in an effort to reassure him, I thought I'd try a little sophisticated conversation. 'You still a virgin?' I asked. That did it. He stood dead in his tracks, glared at me, and then hissed, 'Castrator – castrating bitch . . .' And he ran off, leaving me miles from anywhere, wondering where I'd gone wrong.

I now know, twenty-eight years later, where I did go wrong. My mistake was that I was offering to be a friend, which meant being an equal. There was no way he could accept a relationship like that. I failed in the expected role of a silly little girl who was supposed to need his protection. I could obviously look after myself, and I committed the worse crime of all by refusing to pander to his ego. Why is it, I often wonder, that so many men are afraid their balls are going to drop off and that somehow they end up blaming women for it?

To be a successful woman in any sphere of life is to be considered a threat to men, unless you deliberately monitor yourself and hide your success from both the world and yourself. Millions of women across the globe do just that every day of the year. Jane S., a past patient of mine, had to make a choice at a very early age because she was a clever schoolgirl. She was so alone at school and at home that she became very suicidal. 'She'll grow out of it,' said the local psychiatrist. Jane worked out a strategy of her own. She deliberately failed those exams that were unrelated to her choice of profession, which was accountancy. Apart from working hard in her accountancy course, she became the wildest girl in the school. While the other girls giggled and did each other's hair, she was running around dressed as a boy. If you aren't allowed to beat them – join them, she decided. That was fine during the day, but in the evening when they all went out she'd be sitting at home with the cat.

She worked hard, however, and finally passed all the exams. The boys didn't mind that she had outstripped them because they'd known her for so long that they really didn't think of her as a girl any more. The girls didn't notice her too much; they were too busy chasing the boys, and she wasn't a threat. She was nobody. Her body showed that very clearly. She was like a matchstick and her face was anonymous – a shadow of a human being. After completing schoool she sat down with herself and earnestly decided that she would look for a boyfriend – someone to love her. So she worked out a new strategy: she would try to be like the other girls.

Following that course of action was very difficult for her. She was now at university. Being an accountant meant that she was mostly with men, as there are few women in that profession. She constantly had to make sure that she did not do better than the men she liked. She began to flatter the men around her and to giggle and toss her hair like the girls she used to despise. She found herself joining in with the girls at the university and making friends with them. Most of them were there to get married and to get a degree to use when the children grew up. She used to look with detached amusement at the few girls who were actually there to learn. Although they succeeded academically, they still weren't as clever as she was, for she had learned to play the game, and that meant joining the war.

Her body filled out and her face lit up. She was soon one of the most popular girls there. Men would ask her out and she would go. Long evenings of playing the game – get a man interested, then, as soon as he is hooked, start to torment him. Compare him with other men. Say you would rather be with his best friend. Make him wear different clothes. Throw little tantrums. Above all, keep him sexually titillated. Play the 'I think I'm pregnant' game. Vary that with weeks of no sex. If things are getting a little quiet, spend a few days making him impotent by saying it's his fault you can't have an orgasm. Suggest he visits a psychiatrist and tell him you will go with him. Confuse him by playing at being a little girl when he gets angry, and lapse into baby talk. It's a lethal game when played properly, and men are no match for women who play well.

She married one of the men – the most successful one – because she was best at the game. Everyone came to the wedding. Everyone was crying. She suddenly realised she was crying – for herself. She woke up the next morning beside him and she knew the game was over. She looked at him and decided that she didn't love him. He still loved her. They got a home together and he did well at the bank he joined. She worked for a year, and then they had two children so she left work. They got on pretty well together, except in bed, when she would lie and gaze at the ceiling, wishing it was over and thinking she should be getting paid for it. She pretended she had orgasms and then despised him for not seeing through all that fake moaning and thrashing around. She sat around with her friends, all discussing their men with tolerant amusement. 'Men never grow up,' they would sigh.

The children left home. She decided to go back to work. She never told anyone how she felt about her husband. He was looking puzzled these days. He felt very threatened at the idea of her going back to work. She got a job in an accountant's office, and before long she was asked to be a partner. She would come home exhausted, and then, in an effort to keep up her role as a good wife, she would cook, clean, wash. At work she became more impatient with her colleagues. If there was an office row she would say her piece. If there was a meeting and it was getting bogged down in detail, she would have her say. She realised that the men in the office were feeling threatened. Anger was seeping through the crack in her make-up. She tried to hold back the rage that welled up in her. She went to the doctor, and he gave her Valium and a chat about looking after her husband. She went home and tried to explain to him that she felt she had betrayed herself and him in the process of trying to be what she thought men wanted her to be. She was so confused that she didn't make much sense to herself or to him. He got frightened and called the doctor. 'Nervous breakdown . . . a few days' rest in bed . . . overworking . . . time of life . . .' These words slipped under the door to her room as the doctor comforted her husband. She lay flat on her back and recalled her young self. She had looked for friendships with men, and when she couldn't find that, she did what she saw other girls doing. She could fool everybody else but not herself.

Jane needed someone to listen to her and support her. She worked very hard on herself. She learned to admit to herself that she was brighter than most people and she stopped being ashamed of it. Of course, there were going to be both men and women around, who would see her as a threat. The fact is that there are not many men that can cope with a woman being intellectually more able. She decided she did not have to play a double game. She was going to be herself. At first it caused havoc in her life, but soon she adjusted. Her two boys were delighted. She slowly stopped making herself responsible for everything at home. This meant that she stopped nagging the boys when they were home over every little detail. The place looked less like the local Habitat showroom and more like a home.

Her husband was very unhappy. She wasn't the person he thought he'd married. He felt cheated. True, she seemed much happier. She was less tense, but she kept wanting to talk about 'their relationship'. He didn't want to talk about it. All this talking was dangerous. She started to argue with him in front of guests. She even contradicted him in the middle of a political point he was making. Fortunately, he was able to put things right by correcting her pronunciation before the guests left. Things got really bad. They stopped sleeping together; that was a relief for her. But she felt like a rat in a trap.

At work she became isolated. The men who used to tease her and take her out to lunch stopped. If she was going to be a castrating bitch, then that was her problem. Fortunately there were two other wives in the office who lived their lives as themselves, and she took comfort in their presence. Slowly one of the partners began to spend time with her, first talking about his marriage and its problems, and then listening to her. It took time for both of them to say to each other that they did not want an affair. Having said that, they were both relieved and agreed that they could be friends. Jane was pleased she had a man who was a friend.

The partner's wife was not pleased. Jane was a threat – much more of a threat than if she'd been sleeping with him. Jane tried inviting them both to the house and always being friendly when his wife rang up, but it was no good. Her husband was furious. 'You're jealous,' she said, amazed. 'I don't want to sleep with him. I like him . . . He's a friend . . .' She realised that he didn't allow her a friend; only other women when he was not around, or couples when he was. 'Bitch,' he screamed at her. Then the familiar words 'Castrating bitch . . .'

She looked at him, and she said quietly, like a confession, 'I *was* a bitch and a castrator. I'm sorry I did it to you. But now I am myself. If you want me like I am I'll stay, but if you don't, I'll go.' That night they were kind to each other. They made love, but they cried because they knew it was hopeless and she knew she would have to go.

She had, however, found herself. During the lonely years

that followed she was able to reintegrate her inner self to where she made a life that made sense to her. She decided that she would never compromise in her relationship to a man. She would never let loneliness drive her into the arms of just any man who happened to be around. She had learned that the hard way, after too much wine and a few one-night stands. She also refused to have girlfriends who did nothing but have dinner with each other to discuss the men they did or did not have. A few months of that in the early days convinced her that those women only saw themselves as alive when they were in a relationship with a man, any man. Because they had no self-image, they consumed the man they ensnared. They cannibalised and castrated. She had done it herself and now she had to stay away.

She stopped coming to me as a patient, and then turned up after eighteen months. She looked marvellous. She is a partner in her new firm and makes a lot of money. The boys stay with either parent as they wish. She sings for her local Gilbert and Sullivan company, showing a talent she didn't know she had. There she met a man who is a musician. She loves him and thinks it will work out. I told her I would one day write about the war. 'Tell them about me,' she said, 'and how I gave it up.' 'I will,' I said.

Jane was able to get out and change herself. Many women will recognise the 'Jane' inside themselves. Many men must recognise their fear of women. Then they must come to see women as people in their own right, not as things to be first dominated and conquered, then largely ignored. Men must stop feeling that if a woman tries to offer herself as a friend, she is so much of a threat that she is to be destroyed.

The real castrator, the woman who hates men, doesn't want to change. Buried deep under the fashionable clothes lies a rattlesnake. When any man gets close, she strikes. Her venom smells like perfume, and he doesn't even know he's been struck. Once he is poisoned by her, he spends the rest of his life looking for poisoned relationships. The first woman to strike him is often his mother. These are the men who continue the war with women, who marry, and who, by their behaviour, infect their daughters with the same hatred for men that drove their mothers.

Because Americans are given to making a public fuss long before we do, American women are getting very vocal about the problem of finding a good relationship with a man. They insist it's an American problem. Twelve per cent of American women with university degrees are spinsters. One Washington woman said to me, 'I swim, play squash, read all the newspapers, and eat alfalfa sprouts and brown bread. I have a flat, a sports car and a job I love. I just don't have a man. If I do meet a nice man, he's got at least a hundred other women just like me.' The conversation ended in a long wail. 'At least it's different in England,' she said. 'No it isn't, sister,' I said. It's no different in England, no different in New Zealand . . . I heard the same thing in Bangkok. And for every woman who sits alone at night wondering where all the men are, there is a man wondering where the right woman for him is. The problem is that the war has reached such a pitch that many people opt out and become homosexuals. They say it's safer with your own sex. An estimated thirteen per cent of American men are said to be homosexual. Where does that leave those other women and men who want to be happily related?

We are faced with the onerous task of getting together and discussing what we want from relationships with each other. For years now, it has been radical and chic for women to sit around criticising and complaining about men. Men colluded by being downright hostile and refusing to admit any change was necessary, or by joining men-only groups and loudly announcing it was all their fault and of course women were oppressed. What has never happened is men and women joining together and honestly trying to work out a viable attitude to male/female relationships. There are conferences all over the world on every aspect of family life, but I don't know of one international conference that has ever been held on the expectations that men and women have of each other. Until we know what we want from each other we can't put it right. I believe most of us do want to put it right. I can't be the only one.

(Originally published June 1981, as 'In the battle of the sexes, give peace a chance', reprinted by kind permission of *Cosmopolitan* magazine)

BREAD AND ROSES

'Bread and Roses' never got published. I don't know why. I can see it is not a very polished piece of writing, but then it's a very heartfelt subject. I include it because the whole concept of women being allowed to share in all facets of life is very important to me.

When I began to realise at the late age of thirty that there was more to me than wife and mother, I joined with other women who were reeling from the strident shock waves coming from America and from the pens of women like Jill Tweedie and even earlier, Katherine Whitehorn. We clung together in small groups aghast and angry that we had spent so many guilty years failing to comply with the feminine composite of the 'perfect Persil mum'. Some of us quickly realised that liberation is a word that must be applied to all people, and therefore women cannot be liberated without liberating men. Others took a far more doctrinaire viewpoint, rejecting men as the enemy and turning their back on them.

Many of us changed our ways and in many cases ceased to be closet women. We came out and picked up the reins of our individuality and talent, and began to take responsibility for our own lives instead of remaining in the shadows of our partners and children: the dismissive wife at the office function; the mother perched on the sofa drinking Sainsbury's sherry while the children had their endless parties; the graduate secretary far more able than the boss who writes his reports, makes his coffee with hot milk stirring it before she puts it down before him, spends her lunch-hour doing his shopping, fiddles his expenses for him, and last thing at night sees all his pencils lie sharpened in a pristine row on his desk. No more, said thousands of women ten years ago when three thousand of us marched through London asking for a few very simple demands.

The amazing response was the hostility of men. The subject obsessed most gatherings, and friends were lost overnight when men became so defensive. Conversation was impossible. Women (as in my case) had to be forcefully removed from terraced houses in NW1 when pushed beyond endurance by academically able men with weak egos. No one has ever traced the apocryphal story of the burnt bras; but it remained the base-line for all media jokes and cartoons.

All over the country small cells of women gathered together to discuss and organise a better future for women in the oncoming generations. No longer were we to accept the old rhyme 'Be good sweet maid, and let who will be clever'. I have an address book of that time, and very few of the married couples in it survived the onslaught of the change and upheaval of those years. Many of the male partners paid an unfair price of years of hostility directed personally towards them by their women. Wounded, they retreated and more often than not slipped away to find more conventional, less challenging relationships. The women then found themselves if single mostly alone because male attitudes to women were still extremely patriarchal and the 'Andy Capp' syndrome was no more a working-class laughing matter. The middle-class version merely carried an umbrella and a walking-stick.

Women with children became 'single parents' and gradually from the ashes organisations like Gingerbread were founded – along with countless others – to try to protect women especially when they were at their most vulnerable when they were bearing their children. Still, then as now, women who are child-rearing – the most valuable of all human endeavours – are still the most ignored and derided group in the country. Many women struggled on. Many, having lost the support of a man, merely turned around and searched for another one. Some were lucky and chose a better relationship, having learned from the first round. Many who had little choice simply folded away their dreams and aspirations into the back of their airing cupboards, pushed their Hoovers and thanked

God they were not alone. Success for a liberated woman makes a lonely bedfellow.

For those who chose to fulfil all their ambitions had to realise there was a price to pay.

> 'Do you want to make an author out of a woman? Exactly as if you should announce the project of making your daughter an opera singer when you give her a singing teacher. I say . . . that a woman must never write anything but post-humous works . . . For a woman under fifty to get into print is submitting her happiness to the most terrible of lotteries; if she has the good fortune to have a lover, she'll begin by losing him.'
>
> (Stendhal, *De l'amour*)

Yes, exactly, and not just a writer, almost any other creative or business ability that impinges on the male domain. That's why there are so few women doing it. A lot of women have learned to their cost that there is an old saying: 'Men admire powerful women but they never love them.'

If you look back into the histories of successful women their achievements may shine with a brilliance but in their private lives they most often have the most dreadful relationships with men, except in a few cases where both sides found a compromise like Vita Sackville-West and her husband Harold Nicolson. I don't count the servant/husband relationships because they copy the male model of marrying the office secretary. But I do salute men and women like Beatrice and Sydney Webb (who lived in a house down the road from her), who have a rare and wonderful partnership that has nothing to do with marriage, children or society but is the blending of all that is best in a male responding to all that is great in a female.

It can be creation at its best, whether it's in a slum in Acton or a mansion in Belgravia. It can show itself in the bearing of children who are not crippled and destroyed but grow to their full potential flowering from the warmth of the loving, not unbalanced by either sex seeking to dominate. Or it can manifest itself in all aspects of art. When you are in its presence the possibility of good human relationships makes sense, and many women are beginning to learn that to wait for that possibility may mean a loneliness that can last a possible lifetime or perhaps many years. To ricochet from one man to another can leave a woman's psyche shattered and displace her feeling of self, which is so important if women really want equal relationships with men.

When I was married, and knee-deep in the Refuge, and with my own children, I had given little thought to the problem of loneliness in women who were forging new lives for themselves. It was on my first trip to America that I suddenly found myself faced with the dilemma of women who wished to assert themselves, thereby losing the protective camouflage of manipulating men from the boudoir.

At its most obvious level it manifested itself in the 'Gay' faction of the Women's Movement, which turned its back totally on the male world, lived exclusively in women's communes and preached the new religion with a fervour that was very frightening for the rest of women in the Movement, who wished no ill to their fellow-men, just a loosening of the shackles.

I was travelling with three other Chiswick Women's Aid members and I remember a night when two of us found ourselves being hosted by such a community. Our audience that evening had been exclusively 'gay', and their appearance aped all that women had tried to encourage men to escape. They wore suits and ties and huge boots. They were warm and enthusiastic and felt kindly about us, but for our part, we were terrified by them. My colleague and I spent the night with our suitcases against the door. The one with the cap and sideburns fancied her. She was paranoid about it and wouldn't even offer herself in return for a donation to Chiswick. 'Very unsporting,' I told her as I left her wide-eyed and tense, and went to sleep.

Not all the groups were fanatical and frightening. Many of them quite sensibly said that they needed time to reorientate themselves as women apart from men, to live and work amongst themselves until they felt they knew for sure who *they* were and what *they* wanted, undiluted by the pressure of the male world. Those groups we respected as women coming to terms with their role in the future of our society.

The problem of total aloneness remains for women who still wish to share their lives with men. This was brought home to me when I was with a professor in her beautiful book-filled room. The image still haunts me. She was a warm, exciting, intelligent woman. She suddenly stopped talking about the world-wide position of women, spread her hands expansively and, looking straight at me, said with anguish, 'What am I to do? I've made my way to the top of my profession, I am one of the most popular professors on the campus, but no man will come near me except as a friend. I want to be male-related, I don't want to turn my back on men, but where will I find one?'

I had no answers at all then and very little to offer now except to say that I feel there are several dilemmas for women whose abilities outstrip those of a man's. Either we pay the price in loneliness or we try to encourage men to be less threatened by society's judgemental attitude towards a man's relationship to a more successful woman. Somehow, the worst crime a man can commit is to be seen to take a back seat to his wife. The media are snide, and fellow men are quick to nod and wink. Somehow he is castrated, and his own worth devalued however successful he is in his own field.

If you look back in literature, especially to the great Greek plays, women always did the most ghastly things when they got into any kind of powerful position. The plays were, of course, all written by men. Also, women were portrayed in the past as taking away men's strength, even to the extent of sneaking up to a chap and cutting off his hair when he wasn't looking. No wonder most men sleep so lightly. No, it's no good looking backwards, because we end up with game-keepers (a dying breed these days). Women will have to be the ones to effect a change in their own attitudes to success.

One of the major problems of modern times is that women who wish to fulfil themselves and take up traditionally male-held positions become token males. This is where the hostility begins with men. Both men and women have masculine sides to their natures and at best they complement each other. But when a woman merely develops her aggressive, ruthless, masculine side, out comes a neuter not liked by either sex.

I know it is fair to say that for many women it is the only way they can succeed but the price is too high for them as for all of us. If you look at successful women in all fields of society, many of them have lost all that is warm, generous, humorous and essentially female as opposed to male. However, a woman who at least uses her talents for herself and develops her sense of self, be she ever so lonely, has the comfort of achievement and fulfilment denied to so many of her sisters who cling like ivy to the men in their lives, sublimating all their ambitions for fear of losing him.

How many women do you know who behave like normal human beings until their mate comes into view? Suddenly the sane, mature woman at your side becomes a bad imitation of a local cigarette advertisement. The most damaging are married women with children. Here the mother feels betrayed by society because no longer are the cooking pots the centre of the community life, and her bearing of children merely makes her invisible for years. So she retaliates by pouring her power second-hand into her husband and children. It is a truly dreadful sight as she grows more and more distorted.

The man retaliates largely by retreating to the television/ behind the newspaper/ to his allotment or the pub – so she has only the children to fulfil her own ambitions through. She decides the boy shall be an admiral and the girl will go to Oxford or Cambridge. To this end the girl is conditioned by her mother to see herself as a success only if she is academically successful. This destroys a lot of her intuition and natural femaleness as education is male-based – especially at university level, where logic, the most limiting of ways of thinking, is taught to most students. She is not encouraged to rough-and-tumble with boys but is told to get her degree and marry well, otherwise – it is said without being said, just a tired little smile in the corner of the mouth – 'You will end up like me, sacrificing all I have for you.' Guilt drives the girl into working all hours and achieving neither Cambridge nor Oxford but a redbrick failure followed by pregnancy and marriage. The boy learns to handle his 'difficult' mother and spends the rest of his life looking for 'difficult' women to handle.

The last generation of women had a reasonable excuse in that the end of the war pushed them back into their homes and the pendulum swung away from self-sufficient women to servitude. But we have no such excuse now. It does not mean that many of us may not choose to make raising a family a happy career in itself, but it has to be recognised as a clear choice not a resentment or a contest with one's peer group.

Also, all women must recognise the fact that they will have years on their own when the children are grown up, and prepare for that day with joy. At least the possibilities, especially with Government retraining programmes and the Open University, give women a chance to keep up and to explore more of themselves than ever before.

Maybe it is my generation that will pay the price for women who try to combine all that is best in life. Women who decide to have a child without marriage, or not to have children but to lose themselves happily in a career, must accept at one level a deep sense of loss because running against the accepted mores of any social organisation is painful. I am confident that more women will risk themselves in the future. Remember the mill workers who marched through the streets singing of their dreadfully hard lives, but ended by demanding not just that they bake the bread but that they were entitled to roses, too.

TRIANGLES

I was once the victim of a triangle relationship. It's easy to spot this type of relationship when the people concerned all share the same bed and each other's bodies. It even has a name: 'troilism'. When it's all in the mind it is very difficult to detect. I wrote this article as a warning.

A triangle relationship, at its simplest, occurs when two people form a relationship which is then disrupted by a third person The problem is that the third person causes a serious disturbance. There are, of course, many perfectly healthy relationships where a third party is an asset. An unhealthy situation exists when the third person serves to prevent the original two from having comfortable, honest and happy interactions on their own. The need for such an unhealthy relationship is often hidden deep in the subconscious of the people involved. The triangle resembles the fin of the shark, and is just as deadly.

I suppose I first became aware of this problem when I was at school. My best friend was Dido. She was famous at our school for her athletic ability. Like most schoolfriends, we shared several years of very close friendship. Our first efforts at attracting boys were more to do with our sense of adventure than with actually expecting anything like real interest. In fact, it was Dido who crept out with me one busy Saturday morning and hurled a stink-bomb into the study of a senior boy at the local public school who happened to catch my fancy. As luck would have it, a master was in the room, and returned the cartooned message attached to the stink-bomb to Reverend Mother. Reverend Mother was not amused to see herself caricatured as a bald, hairy-legged, fat little nun. Retribution was swift, for the constant flicker of hell-fire could be seen if one failed to 'own up' immediately. 'Owning up' not only reduced purgatory to several million eons, but also assuaged the eternal sense of guilt built into any good religious upbringing. Fortunately, the boy possessed a sense of humour and sent a clandestine message, which resulted in secret meetings in the woods that surrounded our school.

Michael was great fun, and he, Dido and I spent hours comparing notes on such erotic subjects as school dinners and which prefects were positively beastly. Alas for childhood innocence, the day came when Michael asked me to the End-of-Term Dance. Dido didn't speak to me for days. If she was forced into my company, she spoke only when I made an effort to catch her attention. I was deeply wounded. I assumed she was jealous of me because Michael had chosen me instead of her. I even offered to let her go in my place, but she wasn't interested. We were never close again. You forget as you get older how bitterly hurt you can be by those very vital early friendships. I was always puzzled by her attitude, until years later when I realised that it wasn't me she was jealous of; it was Michael – she wanted me all to herself.

People like Dido are often only children, or children brought up in a family setting in which they have been largely ignored. Children can easily feel ignored either when the parents are very immersed in themselves or when the child is introverted in comparison to brothers and sisters who are boisterous and gregarious. If a person doesn't learn to form easy, sharing relationships in early childhood, it becomes impossible to do so in later life. The result is that any relationship becomes fraught with a painful need to own and to possess.

There are many variations on the triangle theme. I was amazed at the cold, callous way that a merchant banker in his forties decided to solve the problem of his public image. He had always been a homosexual, and had lived with his lover for many years. However, it had been recently suggested to him that it was common knowledge among the directors that he was not a family man, and his future would be more secure if he put this little matter right. He gave the situation a little thought and proposed to a seventeen-year-old society debutante who had impeccable credentials.

They appeared the perfect couple, and the wedding was performed with all the pomp and glitter that a good pedigree and a large amount of money create when joined in holy matrimony. The girl looked enchanting as the organ blared out and she flowed up the aisle on the arm of her handsome, successful husband, who smiled so lovingly into her eyes. Everyone else was dabbing theirs, except for the lover, who didn't look distraught or betrayed, just bored by the the whole thing. I had dinner with the threesome after the honeymoon. The bride still looked radiant. She had totally redecorated their London house, she said, but their main residence would be in Yorkshire. When we sat down at the table I felt it a strange buisness to be sitting between three people who were going to share their lives until death them did part.

'John', she said, smiling at the lover, 'came on our honeymoon. We had such a giggle . . . You should have seen them putting my make-up all over their faces.' She laughed, but there was a strain in the sound. She really didn't know what was going on because she was indeed very young and very over-protected, as only upper-class English girls are these days. The two men had the grace to look slightly embarrassed, and quickly passed on to another subject. So she now lives in Yorkshire and comes to business functions, standing so prettily and loyally beside her recently-promoted husband. He and his lover get on with their real relationship with each other, undetected.

That triangle is quite obvious and will in time probably be exposed. Another sort is often buried in the relationship between two couples. This situation can be infinitely complex. The most common form occurs when a very bored woman wants to have an affair or even to leave her husband, but is too dishonest to admit it. What she will often do is find a man who is sexually attractive and then make great friends with his wife. It is easier if both couples have children, for then she can cement the two families by being absolutely wonderful to the children, who soon spend all their time in her house. The next step is for the four parents to spend long, alcohol-soaked evenings in each other's company. It doesn't take long for the other unsuspecting couple to tell her all their problems. She is wonderfully sympathetic. Soon the other wife gets round to moaning about her husband when they are alone together, and it's not long before the husband (who she is really interested in) comes over after a row to tell her all about it. She gives him lots to drink and warm, loving hugs and kisses, which grow a little longer and a little more lingering as they are alone together. If he get too amorous, she reminds him of her loyalty to his wife and of her total commitment to 'poor Jim', her rather dim but adoring husband. This way, she has the best of both worlds.

She keeps her hard-working, loving husband, who labours like a slave to give her everything she wants. She has a sexually attractive man on the end of a string, who is besotted by her, and she has a girlfriend who she spends all her time with when she is bored. The only way that this destructive triangle is broken is if the other couple suddenly wake up and realise what is happening. They become aware that they never spend time together, that most weekends and holidays are shared with the other couple, that they don't talk to each other any more, that they don't even make love with the same enthusiasm. In short, they realise that they have been taken over.

Wise couples get out. Unwise couples stay in, usually because they need to feed their own bad needs through another person or couple, so the triangle reinforces itself through its angles. The problem here is that very often none of these people behave this way out of choice. Their motivation is deeply unconscious. That is why it is so difficult for them to break it up.

Far more dangerous is the man or woman who knows perfectly well what they are doing as they manipulate another person's life. When I met George, I smelled trouble. At a glance, I would have said that Howard was the problem, but it later became apparent that it was George who was in complete control. Howard was a neat little man, very gentle and musical. He cooked divinely and fussed round George like a mother hen.

George was eternally engaged to my friend Angela. He met her five years ago at her office Christmas party, and lived with her for two years before falling passionately in love with another girl who lived in San Francisco, which meant that he upped sticks and took off, thereby breaking Angela's heart. Twelve months later, he returned to Angela, swearing undying love. All through this travelling trauma, Howard followed George like a faithful and obedient dog. Sometimes Angela would lose patience with the ever-present Howard, but he was always inarguably polite to her, disarming her from confronting him.

Often the two men would arrange to go out to male places – the pub, football matches, and the like – giving Angela the very strong impression that she wasn't included. Angela was so obsessed with George that she avoided any open confrontation with him as well, but she grew painfully aware that there were three of them in this relationship, and that there was no question of Howard moving out.

The fact of the matter was that George steered the relationship for all three, keeping Howard there like a well-trained poodle. If George snapped his fingers, Howard ran. George loved his food, and Howard was forever cooking amazing meals for him. Angela tried to civilise George into at least washing the occasional plate; Howard never expected George to lift a finger. Angela finally lost patience and suggested they should see less of Howard. George reluctantly agreed, and for three months they saw very little of him. But slowly the invitations came through again, and George was back to his old habit of having his cake and eating it.

I realised just how cynical he was one day when we were sitting outside a pub and the weather changed. George looked up at Howard and said he was cold. 'My coat is in the car,' he said. Howard immediately went off to fetch it.

'You sod,' I said. 'You'll never let him go, will you?' George knew I'd seen through the act. All of our mutual friends used to laugh at Howard's devotion, but few saw just how coldly George used him.

George was a self-server of the very worst kind. He knew that Howard was a lonely, very sexually insecure man. George was everything Howard wished he could be. As long as Howard was allowed to crouch at the feet of the master, he was happy. It was a bad relationship for both of them. It made George a domineering user, and it meant that Howard made no effort to form relationships of his own. Finally, George married Angela. Howard was the best man. I refused to go to the wedding. It was doomed before it started.

Very disturbed characters who can't make relationships of their own often pursue people whom they see as life-givers. Healthy people refuse to be put in a triangle position. They make good one-to-one relationships with friends of their choice. The Georges of this world, however, are dangerous to desperate seekers of friendship, whom they use and manipulate as servants. The best analogy I can find is, again, the shark with its pilot-fish. How often do you see these relationships in the office, or among couples that you know? The ever-present, nervously hovering 'best friend' throws himself in as the third corner. If you are on the wrong angle of a triangle, then recognise it and get out. You don't need a partner who wants his share of you and 'A. N. Other' to fulfil his needs. If you have a tendency to act as a triangle-maker, think about the fact that, at the end of the day, the most expendable part of the orchestra is always, indisputably, the triangle-player.

(Originally published December 1981, reprinted by kind permission of *Cosmopolitan* magazine)

YOU TARZAN, ME JANE

The dreadful seriousness of the truly liberated male and his partner was getting under my skin when I wrote this piece. I had met too many men who were cashing in on the Women's Movement as though they had invented the whole business by themselves.

Eddie was the Tarzan of Richmond swimming pool. We mothers lay like sardines round the outdoor pool area last summer, comparing notes on our men and swatting at shrieking offspring. Sometimes we were joined by unmarried friends who had sloped off from the office on a particularly hot day, and then the conversation would widen to include the topic of single men. However, whenever Eddie sauntered through the changing-room door, all conversation would cease and a sigh would run like an autumn wind around the perimeter of the pool.

Eddie was Macho Man right down to the sweat-band on his right wrist. He was also single and very available. Sonia, who usually had no difficulty in catching men, made Eddie her project for that summer.

Sonia was my alter-ego, or to put it less scientifically, she was everything I would like to have been. She was five-foot tall, with long silky blonde hair, and she looked magnificent in a bikini. I was five-foot-six, huge, and my hair looked like a lavatory brush. However, I was good at looking after children, and she excelled in drooping around looking beautiful while holding forth on subjects like 'the meaning of life', and 'Where were all the men she'd read about in the *Standard*?' She was particularly fond of drooping around me because I'd feed her, and because her mind was so occupied with all that philoso-phising that she required someone like me to organise her day-to-day existence. Sonia was a part-time model, spending the occasional night out with an Arab businessman to pay the rent. Her professional life therefore gave her plenty of time to hang around Richmond swimming pool in the summer months. I didn't mind having her around, because I was glad of the company and because her moaning about the meaning of life made a change from the usual moaning about the price of baked beans.

Last summer was a summer of discontent as far as Richmond was concerned, because the usual group had been infiltrated by an unusual newcomer, a woman named Gemma. Gemma looked like a walking advert for the women's page of the *Guardian*. She was deadly serious and had absolutely no sense of humour. Everything about her seemed homemade, including her face. As a matter of fact, everything *was* home-made, down to her shoes. She and her husband even went so far as to recycle their 'waste products' (as she delicately put it) by dumping the fruits of their recycling on their vegetable garden. Quite put us off our packed lunches, seeing her munch her way through her salad sandwiches.

Above all else, it was her attitude to men that got up people's noses. To be precise, the most irritating thing about her was her husband Jasper. Jasper frequently accompanied Gemma, and sat among us at the pool and joined in our conversation. Now, I consider myself as liberated as the next woman, but I drew the line at arguing with Jasper, who considered himself a truly liberated man. After encountering Jasper, I had to re-think my entire attitude to men all over again. I'd just got it all clear in my mind that there were two types of men: the first was Macho Man, who was insensitive, clumsy, only felt at home propping up a bar or watching football, and only came to life in the presence of a woman if she was feeding him or making love to him. If either of those two activities took too long, he was liable to fall asleep. The second type was the Liberated Male – sensitive, intelligent, gentle, loved the company of women, understood them, was sensual and sexually exciting, could cook as well as run a house and manage the children – every-thing I'd always dreamed about and never found. Gemma had one of the second type, and she never stopped talking about him. It was, however, because of Jasper that I had to re-sort these over-simplified categories of men.

Sonia played Jane to Eddie's Tarzan all summer. When they came to my house for dinner, she would drive me potty fluttering around him, seeing his glass was filled, listening to his jokes. She waited on him as if he were a king, an invalid, or an imbecile – I wasn't sure which. He reciprocated by holding doors open for her and by carrying even the lightest of objects that she had in hand. He would try to do the same for me, except I would snap at him because I felt I was betraying my 'sisters' if he so much as opened the car door for me. After the first time I snapped at him, he looked so hurt that I compromised by letting him change a flat tyre once when we were all driving together. It made him happy, and he regained his lost face.

What I absolutely could not tolerate, however, was Eddie's habit of finishing his plate of food, carrying it carefully into the kitchen, putting it into the sink, and then returning to his seat. 'Who do you think is going to wash it up?' I flared.

He looked at me like a hurt spaniel. 'I'm dreadful in the kitchen,' he said. 'All fingers and thumbs.'

'I'll do it,' volunteered Sonia. 'Eddie hates washing up.'

'In my house everyone does everything,' I said firmly. 'No one ever said that a dose of male hormones made it impossible for men to pick up a tea-towel.'

'Here we go . . .' said my eavesdropping son. 'Mum, not everybody wants to be liberated. Some people like the man/woman thing the way it is.' (My son happens to believe that all women should cover their hair and walk ten paces behind their men like the Rasta women. To prove his point he quotes ever-increasing statistics to the effect that thousands of both black and white girls are taking the veil by the minute.)

In the middle of this particular argument, Eddie, in his attempt to help with the washing-up, dropped my Victorian sauceboat. 'I'm sorry,' he whimpered, looking at the scattered pieces. 'The trouble with you is that you should be running around the forests chasing dinosaur,' I said. There wasn't any point in going on. Eddie was Eddie. If I asked him to lift something or to mend something, he would do it gladly. He was wonderful with the children if I could stand the noise of the rough-housing. He treated Sonia like a piece of Dresden, and she loved it.

'How can you?' I asked her, after a particularly long session in a pub where Eddie and his mates played darts all evening and ignored us. 'I don't know,' she said, looking confused, 'but my relationship with Eddie is so simple: we both know where we are.' That seemed to be the most sensitive thing Sonia ever said to me. I went away and decided to really look at Liberated Males like Jasper.

It seemed very calculating to look at one's friends through a microscope, but I was at a time in my life when I urgently needed to reassess some beliefs that I had held in my brain for years. I felt my head was like a huge attic with luggage strewn around, mildewed with age and rust. I seemed to think only in circles, and my biggest block was trying to figure out if there was any hope for men and women to live in peace together.

The turning point for me came when I invited Gemma and Jasper, and Eddie and Sonia for dinner. Jasper arrived carrying a large bowl and a basket of ingredients. 'I'm going to make you a beautiful orange-chocolate pie,' he said, installing himself in the kitchen. I suddenly realised I was furious. I didn't want him in my kitchen. For the first time I understood that *my* kitchen was *my* territory. It dawned on me that for many years I had suppressed this feeling because sexual equality meant that men and women *must* share everything equally, and (I had believed) it just wasn't kosher to say, 'Well, actually, I don't mind you cooking the odd meal if I'm ill or tired, but I don't want anyone to cook on my cooker or to rummage in my knife-drawer or, worst of all, to re-organise my shelves.' My kitchen is myself. It is full of strange smells from past meals and chipped china from forgotten shops. The dog eats from a yellow china plate, and the cats prowl on the counter-tops, picking their way delicately through the mounds of shopping that I forgot to put away. It's very much my place.

It was such a relief for me to say to Jeff, who later came to live with me, 'I prefer to cook,' and for him to say to me, 'I hate cooking. I'd rather wash up.' We both heaved a sigh of relief.

Jasper, however, had tried to take over my kitchen. I looked even harder at him after that incident. Jasper was a perfect composite of so many men I knew in the age-group of thirty to fifty. It was as though the idea of women's liberation came almost too late for them to change internally. Instead, they espoused a cause that they understood intellectually but never emotionally. This way they fooled themselves and hurt a lot of women. Jasper, on the surface, was a wonderful husband and father. Actually he was a bloody tyrant.

Gemma had told me all about Jasper's conversion to the Women's Movement when I first met her. This was the same man who had previously been suspicious of a J-cloth and preferred only to see the children ten minutes before they went to bed. Most of his life was spent in the office, and all of his energy went into waging war against his boss and worrying about the next sales promotion. Gemma was going to a local group and suggested that he stop cracking crude sexist jokes about her activities and read some of the literature. One bored Saturday, he did just that. By Sunday evening, he had been converted.

From the outside, the transformation looked perfect. Jasper, like all converts, became a zealot. He branded himself publicly as a reformed male chauvinist of the first water. He criticised other men in their own homes, pleading with them to change their ways before it was too late. The wives loved him. No longer did Jasper sit with the men and talk about business – oh no. He now sat among the women.

Jasper also discovered touching and hugging. 'Men,' he announced, 'are only sexually aware of women's bodies. They do not know the joy of loving friendships with women.' Jasper was making up for lost time, and when I first knew him, I remember repressing the unkind thought that it was far more difficult to repel Jasper with his asexual hugs and kisses than it was to put off a straightforward sexual grope.

At home Jasper looked over the kitchen and ran the kids' lives. As the children were boys, they were shocked to suddenly find themselves on a housework rota. All war toys were given away. Gemma used to recount all this with an odd mix of smug pride and quiet resignation. By the time of the Orange-chocolate pie episode, I felt there was something desperate in her voice.

Because I was questioning my life-style at the time, I was

probably more perceptive than usual. The end came when Jasper assured me very solemnly in the launderette that he never let Gemma go to sleep at night without her having at least one orgasm. I realised that Gemma had been conned. Jasper stood there in front of the drying-machine looking like a small boy who has just given his teacher an apple. 'How boring for her,' I heard myself say in a cold and hard voice. As his face fell I got angry. I know I didn't say anything coherent. I just yelled and screamed until the lady who does the service-wash came and put her arms round me and gently ushered me to the door. I never spoke to Jasper again, and if I see Gemma I smile. But whatever explanation of my outburst he gave her, he won't have told her the truth. 'It was just Erin having one of her tantrums,' he probably said, knocking up a delicious gazpacho for dinner. 'Pity she never really understood a man's relationship to the Women's Movement.'

The fact is, I do understand it, only too well. I watch my friends who blossomed in the early days of the Movement and then withered as the men they knew shifted their power-base. If women were going to demand equality and the sharing of roles then, by God, that's what they were going to get. Men moved in and took over. Gone were the days when a woman ran her home and steered the family life, wishing her man would help a little now and then. With the ruthless cunning of the power-hungry male, he totally moved into her territory under the guise of sharing. She woke up to find herself colonised in the last bit of female territory left to her – her home.

Gemma will never see Jasper's 'conversion' as typical of a narcissistic self-server. The truth is, however, that Jasper didn't change; he adapted himself. Gemma won the war in public. Her man is a fervent supporter of her cause. Gemma now lives with a man who is a perfect housewife and mother. As he flits about with his pinny and his rubber gloves, he looks just like his mother. I'm not surprised she doesn't fancy him much. Men like Jasper need a Government Health Warning tattooed on their foreheads: 'This man causes brain damage.'

Those of you who have read this article so far must be feeling suicidal. Please refrain from ending it all. Yes, there are thousands of men like Jasper, and there are thousands of women like Gemma who get taken in and are eventually destroyed. If it's happening to you, now is a good time to get out. But for the many men who really do want to live more comfortably with a woman and to be less of a stereotype than Eddie, there are plenty of waiting women. For all that one can describe a shift in social attitudes and chart its effect on the psychological and political life of a country, people area individuals, and as such, it is their own personal history that shapes their destiny.

Michael was lucky, I thought. He had had a really warm family as a child. His mother ran the sort of house all children dream about. It was comfortably untidy with dogs and cats all over the place. Being a convent girl, I was horrified when one of the slobbery boxers got loose and was mating in a very inelegant fashion in the front garden with another of the family's dogs. Michael's father got a large pail of water and doused both dogs. I was mortified, only to find that the whole family spent the next two hours discussing mating techniques in the breeding of dogs. Sex in his house didn't lurk in the woodshed.

His mother was a large, untidy woman who was a part-time teacher at the local primary. His Dad was employed as an insurance clerk – a job which he hated – but his real love was his workshop, where he pottered for hours. Mike's Mum and Dad cuddled (again very embarrassing to me). After a few pints, his father would sing to her. There were four children, and they seemed then, as they do now, to be incredibly lucky.

Michael became a probation officer and married Annie, who is a quiet, reserved girl with a wonderful sense of humour. I know that Michael often talks about men's attitude to women. I suppose he saw his father help his mother round the house as a matter of course, not as a political gesture. The strong and very apparent bond between his parents gave him a model for his own choice of a partner. He didn't have a very damaged background to come to terms with, so it was easier for him than for many of us. Of course, I must remind myself that it is the extremes that one tends to remember and to write about. It is easy to forget to acknowledge those relationships where the men are happy and well-adjusted. It is those men like Michael who will produce the next generation of sensitive, adjusted children. If I feel low at times, after a week of nothing but hearing about awful problems, I go and see them.

The final hurdle for me was to come to terms with the fact that a lot of attitudes I'd been preserving were kept alive largely because I didn't dare admit to myself that life is never black or white. It is a never-ending, ever-dissolving shade of grey. For all that I intellectually wished that men could be more like women, physically I liked men to be male. I now feel that men and women each need to retain an air of uncharted territory. Part of a man should still be that which is male and 'other', not totally understandable – a mystery. The endless quest to understand is exciting. To force one sex to become like the other is to create a mutant gender. When it comes right down to it, in the jungle of life Jane needs her Tarzan.

(Originally published September 1981, as 'Can Tarzan change his spots?', reprinted by kind permission of *Cosmopolitan* magazine)

TEN YEARS ON

Deirdre McSharry asked me to write an article for the celebration of *Cosmopolitan*'s ten years of existence. As usual I got totally carried away and off the point. It didn't get published because it's not a good piece of journalism. I include it because I would like to look back in ten years time and see how much of a fool I made of myself.

When I first discussed the possibility of writing an article to commemorate *Cosmopolitan*'s first decade, the Editor suggested that I might look at the ten years to come. My initial instinct was to wonder if anyone would be alive to actually read it. Deirdre, however, revived me with a glass of Californian wine and positively refused to listen to my lecture on how the San Andreas Fault would cause California to slide into the sea, thereby making this particular glass of wine historic. 'Life,' said the indomitable editor, 'will go on.'

Glowing with such positive assurance, I took myself off to a bookshop and collected an armful of books on the subject of the future. Then, bleary-eyed from all that reading, I repaired to the Psychics and Mystics Fair, which was held at Alexandra Palace. Financially twenty pounds lighter, I left with a list of prophecies for the years to come. Still searching, I asked a Buddhist friend to consult the Tibetan Lamas at the Manjushri monastery in the Lake District. I was given a fascinating booklet by a man calling himself 'a futurist'. Finally, I consulted women friends, most of whom are deeply involved in their work in the fields that most concern women.

Putting it all together, I see the next decade as the 'dark decade'. It is irresponsible not to take the threat of nuclear war very seriously. The next decade will decide whether or not nations can learn to co-operate with each other instead of threatening to wipe each other out. Certainly, there will be a very real danger that Israel will be the victim of a nuclear attack, which will rid the Middle East of an intractable territorial problem and allow the two superpowers to have waged war at another country's expense.

Having said all that, I find the most comforting thing about considering our future at all is the ancient saying 'Danger itself fosters the rescuing power'. So, although the next ten years will be dark and dangerous, by 1992 I expect to see a growing renaissance and a time of great happiness. I believe it is during this dreadful time that women will finally come into their own.

Ever since men took control from women, the world has slowly degenerated into chaos. Thousands of years ago, women were responsible for the care and maintenance of the community. Religion, fertility, childbirth, care of the hearth and the home, were all her domain. Not that those functions were seen as second-rate pastimes; indeed, in those times people lived under the 'feminine principle'. The moon was worshipped as a goddess, and her waxing and waning were seen as the major religious influences of that time. Women were powerful, and their attributes were seen as a life-giving force to be saluted and respected.

With the advent of the most primitive technology that freed men from the hunt, which previously had taken them away for many moons for their communities, the cult of the feminine principle was slowly eroded. Men began to assume the roles traditionally held by women, right down to engineering and controlling the very moments of her giving birth. Slowly all that was once rounded, warm, receptive, intuitive and fertile became lost in the mists of time. Matriarchy was dead. Instead, the world became patriarchal, and in their race for technology, men learned to fear the force of the mother moon and her daughters, denying them their equal role. Men knew that women care little for sterile machinery and phallic warheads.

1971 saw, however, the rebirth of the Women's Movement in England. Even though it arrived with screams of rage, I can remember the first exhilarating march for women and the tremendous feeling of power it engendered. We were no longer helpless creatures fettered to our kitchen sinks. From 1971 to 1981 enormous strides were made in the public consciousness of how women had been oppressed and discriminated against. I don't believe that there are any women in this country who haven't at some time in those ten years seriously looked at themselves in the light of the huge social changes that shook the foundations of our society. The Seventies were the years of anger. It was a necessary anger to forge a new reality that could look ahead and create an equal space for men and women to live in peace together.

Technology will continue to run its course. This means that during the next ten years, women will come to terms with the Computer Age. Far from being afraid of the mathematical concepts used in scientific programmes, they will find that the new technology is ideally suited to the intuitive and cognitive abilities that women naturally display. Those women who wish for a career in management will find that they will be freed from the traditional secretarial roles, and will be able to take their place at the management table. Certainly, it will be up to women already in senior management positions, and educators, to see that young girls are encouraged to use computers and become familiar with the revolution that is taking place in the office.

Dark futurists are predicting that offices will become nothing more than vertical filing cabinets linked to workers' houses, where they will crouch over their home word-processers with a telex in the toilet. However, those futurists forget that the creative process that underlies all ventures – be they financial enterprises or forms of communication such as magazines – will always require the coming together and com-muning of creative souls. What will be liberating is the fact men and women who do want to stay at home during their children's early years will no longer need to be cut off and isolated from the mainstream of life. They will indeed be able to remain at home and either link in with their old jobs and continue to work part time from home, or enjoy some of that time pursuing further studies. Allied to this facility will be the freedom from shopping for day-to-day items and a reduction in household chores, for within the next ten years, dusting, hoovering and all other forms of housework will have become automatised mechanical processes.

All these advances will leave the way clear for pursuing alternative ways of living that enable a woman to fulfil herself without a permanent relationship with a man. In the next ten years 'shared living' will become a much more normal way of life. It will begin with the huge numbers of women – and some men – who are single-parent families either by design or by accident. They will demand that they should not remain totally vulnerable at the bottom of the social scale because of their commitment to their children. Designs are even now in existence for shared-living housing schemes for single-parent families. These schemes will provide an alternative for those women who, for one reason or another, do not want to live in a nuclear-family setting and feel happier in a communal situation.

They will completely revolutionise modern council estates, which will cease to be built as ghettos, but will reflect the urge for all sections of the community to live interdependently side-by-side. Even though shared living will begin largely through the efforts of women, men too will come to see the advantages and will happily choose to share in community life – many of them relieved at the idea that they can partake in 'family life' without necessarily having to create their own.

Every time an advance is made, alongside it should come awareness of the need to destroy the dreadful myths that have long bedevilled both sexes. The 1980s will have to be a time of great honesty because the threat of an ultimate war will cut away so much of the hypocrisy that has surrounded us.

Certainly, I feel that the political situation will become so acute that by 1986 we will see a completely new form of government, which will revolutionise Parliament, throwing out all the old masculine traditions. By this time, women will have asserted themselves as politicians, and it will be their influence that will formulate a central government which will have individual members of Parliament chosen by their constituencies for their personal intregrity and leadership. I predict that they will serve a three-year term and then stand for re-election. There will be a manifesto drawn up by each government which will be adhered to by all members of government because it will reflect the wishes of the public, who will be closely consulted. Many women will be appointed to positions of great power both here and abroad.

By this time, the battle to wrest childbirth from the male-dominated medical profession will have been won, and though men who wish to serve in maternity hospitals will be welcomed, there will be almost no place for the regimented machine-operated deliveries that we suffer now. Women will demand and take responsibility in those areas that they enjoy, but there will be an easy interchange between those women who wish to enter traditional male fields, and men who will be less threatened with the new liberalised attitude to sex roles.

The medical and psychiatric stranglehold on the country will be breached, partly because new alternative medical care based on the *prevention* of disease will be seen to be more effective. Natural alternative medical remedies are less harmful to the human body, and as the boundaries between science and religion recede, faith healing will become accepted. There will be a huge spiritual regeneration taking place, because people will be looking outwards, and many will be badly shaken by the events that will occur in the next ten years. The Church in this country will open its doors to the influences of Eastern religions, and people will come back to hear the messages that they have so long ignored.

The next ten years are going to be a very exciting time to be alive. Women, who are natural communicators, will find that with all the new openings in television, radio and video, many opportunities will present themselves for them to shape and influence the thoughts and aspirations of this decade. The 1980s will be politically and financially difficult, but with the hope and faith of all people in this country, it will also be a time of great regeneration. March 1982 is an auspicious time for *Cosmopolitan* to have its tenth birthday.

IT'S ALL IN THE CARDS

I have been reading the Tarot cards for years. It's a marvellous way of meeting people! So I wrote this article to encourage shy people to find a way to communicate with other people and to enjoy such an ancient and historically interesting craft.

It was after dinner that I was asked to bring out 'my cards'. Both women with me were married and were friends of mine. The older woman asked me to do hers first. I began to lay them out when the card of the lovers appeared. Without thinking I said, 'Helen, you didn't tell me you are having an affair!' Helen went purple, her friend looked aghast and the three of us stared at each other. 'How did you know . . .?' she said when she finally got herself together. I showed her how the cards lay, and said that I was as embarrassed as she was. After all, I had always known her family as happy and secure, so it came as quite a shock. They both left fairly quickly after that, and she has never been comfortable in my company since. I learned a big lesson from that night: Don't play with the cards if you don't want to hear what they might say.

Some women pick up a needle and they can sew. For some, it's knitting. I was always hopeless at those skills, but from the moment I bought my pack of Tarot cards, I felt I had owned them all my life. I am an Aquarian, and most Aquarians take an enormous interest in anything to do with the occult. Certainly, I had always been interested in astrology and was forever seeking out old ladies on the end of Brighton pier who would assure me my life would be full of tall, dark, strange men. They were right, but the men usually turned out to be the milkman or the central-heating engineer.

One day, in the company of a Pisces lover, we had our fortune told by a woman who owned a deck of Tarot cards. From that moment I knew I had to find my own pack. Within days, I had tracked down the particular type I wanted. There are at least twelve different designs of Tarot cards. I think everyone should choose the pack that they are most comfortable with. This means finding somewhere like the Compendium Bookshop (at 234 Camden High Street NW1, who keep a large stock) and getting the feel of the different packs and designs. I chose the Aleister Crowley pack, plus a book called *The Definitive Tarot* by Bill Butler, and retired home to practise.

It was an eerie experience to hold a pack of cards knowing that less than two hundred years ago I would have been burnt to death for just owning them. These cards are said to have been first written about in 1392, and have come from the Mahatmas of Tibet, or from the gypsies, or from the Kabbala. I didn't even have to study very hard; I felt so at home with all the symbols that I didn't need to look them up. It fascinated me to lay them out with all their practical day-to-day meanings like loss of money, love, interference, indolence, disappointment, and the powerful cards of death and regeneration, or the card of ruin which warns of total destruction. The more I worked with them, the more I understood the meanings within the meanings. I was an awful bore for the first few weeks. I really didn't want to be with people – I just wanted to be alone to play with my cards.

I was booked to take a holiday in Greece for the first time in my life. Setting out, I was very nervous as I had just separated from my husband after seventeen years of marriage, so going anywhere as a single woman was an ordeal. I needn't have worried – my cards saved me. From the moment I took out my Tarot cards in the family taverna at my Greek campsite, I was inundated.

I had timidly wondered about practising my cards on unsuspecting friends, but here I had a ready and waiting clientele. Soon I had reassured Papa Milonas that his money worries were only temporary, and Mama that the goats would give birth safely. I was then plunged into the intricacies of the son Mavrantzis' love life. 'Much problem,' I admonished him.

He beamed. 'Women no problem,' he said. He regretted it. Twenty-four hours later we all leapt from our sleeping bags as someone went berserk with a shotgun. I saw Mavrantzis a bit later. In had been an angry Greek father protecting his daughter's virginity. 'Problem,' said Mavrantzis. I nodded sagely.

By now, word had got round the island of Zakinthos, and droves of Greek families – particularly the women – came up to the campsite to have their cards read by 'Madame'. I didn't speak any Greek, so an awful lot of it was pure pantomime. After a skinful of ouzo I could read anybody's cards. I came back to England having had the holiday of a lifetime.

Actually, once you have settled down and are over the first thrill of divining the meanings of the cards, it can all get out of hand. I've done the cards for a lover, only to find that they prophesied that he'd leave me for another woman within the next few weeks. 'Actually,' he said, 'I've been meaning to tell you . . .'

The other problem is that once people know you do the cards, you begin to wonder if they've come to see you as a friend or if they are actually waiting with ill-concealed impatience until they can legitimately ask you to produce the things. After a while, it can get very wearing, because whatever country you are in, whoever you are with, the main question you are always asked to answer is, 'Who will love me?'

My cards travel everywhere with me. I've done the Tarot in Alaska and in New Zealand. I've done the Tarot in a hotel in Calcutta where the whole place was 'dry' and I couldn't get a drink. Once the word spread that I was doing the cards, the supply of alcohol sent up to my room was unlimited. I've even wheedled my way over unfriendly Yugoslav borders. As the guards glared into the windows of our motorhome this summer, I laid the cards on the table. They had been ransacking the people in front of us, but one look at the graphic cards of death and destruction meant they muttered superstitiously to each other and waved us through.

I honestly don't believe that the cards hold any inherent magic within themselves. What you can do is to use them to touch the unconscious wishes and needs within yourself and other people. I find that the more aware I am of my own inner world the more accurately I can link into the world of the person sitting in front of me. In the hands of an irresponsible person the cards could be dangerous, but only because they could be used to manipulate or terrorise vulnerable people. For that reason anyone wishing to use the cards should be aware of why they want to use them. Also, anyone wishing to have the cards read for them should choose someone they trust, or someone who has some reputation in that field. If you do decide that you would like to own the cards, you have my best wishes, and I hope they give you many hours of happiness.

(Originally published January 1982, as 'Erin Pizzey sets out the Tarot cards', reprinted by kind permission of *Cosmopolitan* magazine)

WHAT DID YOU DO
IN THE OFFICE TODAY?

The frustration of ten years of waiting for my husband to come home at night to give me news of the outside world went into this article. I felt better once I'd written it, and so did all the other women who wrote in to agree with me.

'What did you do in the office today?' All over the world, weary women wait for the front door to open every evening only to ask their equally weary man that question. Usually he says, 'Nothing much,' and she masks her anger at being denied her one life-line to the outside world with cheerful chatter about the children. He hides his guilt at denying her information about his day, and feels desperately that he needs at least half an hour to separate the office reality, where he is the wage-earner, from his evening role as husband and father. He sometimes feels his family are like vultures, waiting to pick him clean when he comes home.

A different problem exists for two people who are both working equally hard outside the home, and then come through the front door together. At least, where a wife is home with children and the man is the wage-earner, their roles still retain some vestiges of clarity. But for the couple who are equal earners, there is as yet no clear book of rules as to who pays what or unto whom. Even more fraught is the question of whose responsibility it is to wash/cook/clean and put out the cat.

There are a lot of cowardly women in this world who work full-time and then go home and play total housewife. They're on a hiding to nothing, because the sort of man who demands that kind of service tends to use his wife to aid him as he climbs to the top of his particular professional tree, and then move on to a younger woman, a 'new, improved model', only to use her in the same way. You can usually pick these women out at the back of the office typing-pool, looking fifteen years older than their age, with their eyes moist with tears from crying over lost opportunities.

Apart from anything else, if a couple can't sort out reasonably fair roles for themselves, then they have not arrived at any real basis for a relationship. The most contentious arguments always arise over the minor issues. The first argument often is about who gets the shopping. It is usually assumed by even the most caring of men that his job carries so much more status that shopping during the lunch-hour should naturally be done by the woman of the family. Besides, a woman (be she the editor of a magazine, no less) is not a figure of fun if she has a carrier-bag loaded down with Persil and cat-litter. But her male equivalent would probably have to sneak through a side-door and hide the same objects until it was dark enough to slip into the night.

The awful reef that damages so many working couples is the paying of bills. Money is always a totally irrational subject, and its proper handling depends upon the maturity of the couple involved if they are to share their incomes without rancour. Things become difficult when the man earns more than the woman. This again can put pressure on her to contribute more by way of housework.

The other problem is how much of each individual's office life should be shared with their partner. Working couples usually have equally intense office lives. Unless they share an absorbing hobby, the evening tends to be a time when they both need to let off steam. That's fine, if they are both intensely verbal extroverts who spend hours dissecting each other's office relationships and intrigues. But we all tend to choose our opposite, so you often get the woman pouring out her heart to an introverted male who lets his day float away while he immerses himself in the *Standard*.

The answer for most working couples seems to be the drawing up of ground rules. It's best to begin with all the dreadful irritations that bedevil a relationship which should be loving and fulfilling. It takes give on both sides. If he is a messy inconsiderate brat, don't blame him – blame his mother. Look at it as a salvage job. On the other hand, if he's anally and compulsively neat and you are not, he'll blame your mother.

You must both sit down and work out a reasonable rota. The main thing with a rota is to allow for 'swaps'. If you don't feel like lugging the laundry to the launderette, swap him for the job he least likes. After a while the rota tends to adjust itself.

One couple I know decided that rather than part, they would spend a tenner a week on a cleaning woman who at least did the worst of the hoovering and mucking out of the rooms. It was the best decision they ever made, because in the evenings, they come home now to each other, not to a mighty war over the washing-up.

It is worth a look at two couples more closely to see how they came to terms with their relationships. I was interested in a girl named Pat whom I met at a dinner-party. She regaled me with hilarious stories of her escapades as an air-hostess. I didn't realise that she was with a man until she was leaving on his arm. He seemed much older and very quiet. What an odd relationship, I thought. I wondered if they shared anything at all together. I remember feeling puzzled.

I met Pat again and she asked me round for a drink. She and Bob lived in a little terraced house in Fulham. I was struck by the peace they shared between them. Pat was a really elegant woman. I asked her why she chose to be an air-hostess instead of a model. She said she loved to fly and to travel, and she was so senior in her job that she always got the best flights. Because I am always incredibly curious, I did get round to asking her about her relationship. 'Doesn't he mind you flipping all over the world?' 'No,' she explained. He had been married, and his first wife had resented his passion for gardening and his absorption in books and music. He ran a small family wine firm. Pat had been with him for five years when I met her. They were as different from each other as chalk is to cheese, and they were happy. They had discussed from the beginning their own attitudes to their life-styles. Their views fitted in nicely, and they were happy to stay together without marrying.

Pat's father was a missionary, and her childhood was spent traipsing around the world with her mother, following her father, who had usually moved on and left a series of instructions as to which native village he was currently converting. It would be possible to say that Pat had chosen a father-figure in Bob, but that would be far too facile an explanation.

Here were two people, each with a very strongly defined sense of self. Both of them had internal resources that gave them much private pleasure. Bob had his books and music as well as his garden, which he preferred to experience alone. Pat was not much interested in any of those things, but she had a passion for photography which kept her locked away in a dark-room for hours and hours.

They did once go on holiday together, but it was a disaster. Bob behaved like a drug-addict without a fix if he couldn't get to a piano, and Pat spent her entire time leaning over crevices looking for the right angle for the perfect shot, or stalking the local peasants with a telephoto lens. Bob dreamed of his study and a bottle of Châteauneuf-du-Pape '79 instead of the domestic axle-grease he had in front of him, and Pat was so excited by the sunrises that they had no time to make love. She would either be leaving to catch the moon waning, or returning to describe the sunrise to a sleepy and disgruntled Bob.

They both agreed that their happiest times were spent when they were at home together, but each could withdraw into their private worlds without threatening the other. I found it interesting that they faced quite a lot of hostility from other people, who felt threatened by the freedom they gave to each other. I loved them both and could spend time with Bob in the garden watching him grow marvellous vegetables like magic, or I could trot round after Pat as she swept through South Molton Street looking for a silk blouse in exactly the right shade of blue to go with her Yves St Laurent suit.

They did very much compartmentalise their lives. Certainly Bob would not have casual relationships, but he recognised Pat's need for freedom, and said from the beginning that he would never question her. Quite honestly, she was not the sort of woman who gossiped about her private life, but I suspected that she did have casual relationships when she travelled – but nothing that would harm their tranquil long-term love for each other.

Sue and Peter, however, took a lot more sorting out. If you

marry as a lie, it's so hard years later to admit it to each other. Actually, Sue was attracted to all the wrong parts of Peter's personality. She married him because she wanted desperately to be as gregarious as he was. She never felt she had enough character to go out there and be the centre of attention, but through Peter she would be included. In order to achieve her emotional needs, she set out being the perfect wife, mother and hostess. Susan was dreadfully insecure, and Peter, who was forging ahead in his insurance company, soon found himself trapped. Their first rows occurred very early in their marriage, when her habit of telephoning him in the office began to make the other staff tease him about having a suspicious wife. She was soon pregnant and became very depressed.

Peter was out many nights going to clients' homes, which meant she would insist on waiting up for him. He would come in tired, after a heavy evening of persuading a reluctant client to take out insurance, only to find Susan in tears, accusing him of being unfaithful. Peter didn't have time to have affairs – not then, anyway. Susan seemed to Peter to want to share in every little thought of his.

After the first child, she took to entertaining in a big way. She realised that she couldn't extract much information out of Peter, so she threw herself into a social life. Peter was pleased at first. He was waiting for promotion and could do with all the help he could get. Certainly, Sue was an excellent cook and catered very well, if you could stand the nervous strain she was putting herself through. What Peter hadn't bargained for was that Sue wasn't really interested in furthering his career. She was furious when I pointed this out.

Her main aim was to get herself into his office life. Before long, various colleagues would be dropping by the house, knowing they'd be warmly welcomed by Sue and, at first, by Peter. However, it was a large staff with plenty of hot, juicy office gossip going round. There was Sue, taking it all in and, before long, running her own little therapeutic community, though it was not at all therapeutic for her relationship with Peter. Peter found out that he really resented not having his office life to himself. He didn't want to come home at night to yet another of his colleagues (mostly female) sobbing all over Sue, drinking his hard-earned gin. Sue retaliated when he complained by asking him how he could deny all that they meant to each other by insisting on a life of his own that did not include her.

Peter slammed out of the house feeling angry and guilty. He stayed away for two days. Then, overcome by guilt and remorse, he went back. They both promised each other they would try again. She said she would interfere less in the office, and he promised to make an effort to be home more. They had another child because Peter thought it would keep Sue busy, and Sue wanted another child because she was terrified of losing Peter and because he was always most attentive when she was pregnant.

The baby arrived, and so did the post-natal depression, for they both had slowly slipped back into their previous patterns of behaviour. She started to phone Peter at the office again, and Peter began to come in later and later. Sue felt he had another woman. This time she was right. He did.

The problem was that their marriage was over as far as Peter was concerned. The truth was that he couldn't take much emotional responsibility for anyone, certainly not to the extent that Sue required. He felt happy when he had his life in well organised compartments. He had his office life. There, he was the rising young businessman, well-dressed, always cheerful and very much a favourite with the secretaries. At the sports club he had a good backhand for tennis, and played an aggressive game of squash. In the pub he knew about beer, and told his jokes for his friends. Then – and it did come at the end of the list – there was his home, where he retreated. He liked to feel that it was his lair and that he could foray out into the world alone, very much the predatory male with his safe place always there and waiting.

Unfortunately for Sue, he found a woman who would do just that: she was there when, and only when, he wanted her. She was a woman who also liked to keep her life in compartments. She would let Peter loose because she didn't mind too much if he didn't come home. She'd been married before and, I think it was really the status of being married that was important to her. So, in choosing Peter, she chose a cat that wouldn't disrupt her life. This suited both of them. But Sue was devastated.

They divorced, and Peter immediately remarried. Sue had a difficult time coming to terms with Peter's rejection of her. Gradually, though, she began to realise that she didn't need to live through someone else, but was perfectly capable of being the centre of attention herself. All she had to do was to risk herself a little.

It was three years before she met a man who seriously interested her. It was a good choice for both of them because he ran a bookshop and very much wanted a wife to work with him. It was nice to see Sue so happy. Because this man was capable of a really deep emotional relationship, Sue didn't feel threatened if he did go off to buy books, or to London for a few days. She realised that her clinging to Peter had been a symptom of her subconscious knowledge that Peter was never a 'safe place' for her. Her marriage to Peter had been unlike the relationship between Bob and Pat, whose safety in each other was never questioned by either of them.

I honestly believe that in a relationship you can either work together or totally separately, depending on your own personality. It all goes wrong when people use a place of work or other interests to hurtfully exclude the other partner. Women are most likely to be victims of this exclusion, because for many years they will suffer the isolation that society imposes on them when they stay at home. The man then tends to become their only link with the outside world.

My first marriage meant a lot of time on my own. It also gave me plenty of time to think. I feel that I am a person who needs to work and share with my partner anything I'm doing. I often think this wish to share everything stems from the fact that I am a twin and have been used to a very close relationship since birth.

Now, in my second marriage, Jeff and I work together. Whether we are at the Refuge or writing books or articles, we like each other to be there. However, I know many couples who are just as happy as we are who would hate to live like that. The secret is to know yourself well enough to be realistic about your choice of relationship. If you like to share everything you do with your partner, and he does too, it will be a beautiful duet. If, on the other hand, you insist on choosing a man who likes to compartmentalise his life, unless you like to live the same way, his compartments could become your coffin.

(Originally published March 1982, as 'When will women ever learn?' reprinted by kind permission of *Cosmopolitan* magazine)

IS IT BETTER TO HAVE LOVED AND LOST?

This was just the sort of article I would write after having comforted yet another girlfriend. In fact, this is dedicated privately to my sister, who is far more sensitive than I am but is learning to take risks.

Is it better to have loved and lost than never to have loved at all? It's the sort of question you ask yourself when you're sitting on your bed, having just finished a good howl, clutching a wad of Kleenex. A large part of the wardrobe is empty, from where he has decanted his clothes, and the bathroom looks alien without his spread of shaving gear and dropped socks. Losing a lover is *the* most painful happening in most people's lifetime. It is one thing that happens to almost all of us, and there are no provisions to help anyone through the agony of it all. Most people rely on their friends, but the truth is that friends can only take so much of the pain, and then they back off. Somehow if a woman is widowed she has more sympathy, even though that is fairly limited. But if your man has gone out of your life, the attitude is usually 'Pull yourself together', or 'There are plenty more fish in the sea.'

Actually, I had a great deal of sympathy for a girlfriend who said she would far rather he had dropped dead, because although she would have been grief-stricken, at least her pain wouldn't have been sharpened by the acute agony of knowing he was still on the same earth, and was now in someone else's life. It was precisely this emotion which made women all over the world empathise with the headmistress in Scarsdale, New York, who shot her lover to death rather than lose him to another woman. Even though she was jailed for life, I suppose she will take a grim satisfaction in knowing at least that no one else can have him.

I have known several women who have killed their men. At the bottom of all their motives was the fact that he was leaving them. They were all women who were unable to bear the betrayal because they had invested all of themselves in their relationship to one man. For everyone, a large part of being left is a feeling of murderous rage, which can be quite frightening for someone who has never come across the violent potential in their own personalities.. The only comfort in these situations is to reckon that most people do survive a broken love affair and go on to try again.

I have come, however, to the conclusion that there are three distinct categories of women: the first is the 'no-risk-taker', the second the 'occasional risk-taker', and the third is the 'disastrous risk-taker'.

The first type, the no-risk-taker, is really someone who often seems to have all life's problems sorted out. Everyone goes to her because she is so level-headed and sympathetic. In fact, she is probably a roving resource centre, open to the public twenty-four hours a day. Her flat is always full of waifs and strays. Errant husbands sleep on her lumpy sofa when they can't face a row with the wife. Her spare bedroom usually has a couple of teenagers on the run from over-zealous parents. Her kitchen is her confessional, and her wooden table is scarred from tears and cigarette ash.

'Great girl,' everyone says, but where does all this leave her? Exhausted. So she lectures everyone on the virtues of universal love, or explains that her life-style is her primary relationship and, therefore, she is happy to be alone. Actually, I think all that is just an excuse to avoid taking the risk of getting hurt.

I remember talking to George, who fell in love with just this sort of no-risk-taker. He said it was like storming the Bastille. Even getting to talk to her was a major manoeuvre because her running a home-made drop-in centre meant that he had to push his way through piles of people. He finally invented a hideous non-existent problem to catch her attention. This ploy worked in only a limited way, for she would hold his hand all moist-eyed while he told her of his terrible problems with women, but the moment he got on to the subject of her lovely blue eyes, it was like approaching an iceberg. He finally gave up, which was a great shame because women like that are so alone. They are like cadavers on a heart-machine. Most people experience the highs and lows of life, knowing that the highs will make the suffering of the lows all seem worthwhile. No-risk-takers, however, in their absolute fear of ever risking a low, will also never feel the joy of life's highs.

Often I find these women afraid of everything that a relationship offers – not only the intimacy of sex, but also the sharing of their inner self and private space. It can become far easier to live on their own, enjoying the self-indulgence of their own space and their own timing rather than undergoing the discipline of making room for the needs of another human being.

It is also the no-risk-taker who usually has had a careful and studious childhood. Encouraged by possessive and over-protective parents, she then marries the first available no-risk man. Together they fail to grow or change, always living on the periphery of other people's lives. I honestly find this sort of man or woman very sad. So often they defend their way of life with a great deal of anger, because part of them would so much like to burst out and join the rest of us messy, inadequate human beings.

The occasional risk-taker is what most people are. We all know what we are supposed to look for in relationships. We have been brainwashed by our mothers to grow up to 'marry well', and that can mean anything, depending on one's mother's personal fantasies. My mother opted for a doctor for me and an admiral for my sister. Needless to say, we both failed her. But occasional risk-taking meant that in between the search, we strayed off the straight and narrow into the arms of the unsuitable, and therefore faced some ultimately painful experiences.

My heart was first broken when I was fourteen, and my best friend's brother took another girl to a dance instead of me. On hearing the dire news the next morning, I put my head down on my desk during Latin and howled. I swore that never would any man hurt me so badly again – not too difficult a promise, as I was locked away in a convent at the time. However, the second heartbreak came when I was eighteen and my mother caught me on the station trying to elope with Pierre. He saw her, and hopped on to the train alone instead of wresting me from her possessive arms.

In the middle of the family screams and recriminations that followed, I remembered the familiar feeling of that very singular pain that one feels when one human betrays another. It is interesting that pain has very different dimensions. The pain of childbirth is so different from the pain of disease. So, too, the pain of a death is different from the pain of the death of a relationship. People's capacity to feel pain also varies enormously. That is why an event will affect different people in different ways.

Certainly, the occasional risk-taker will feel pain, which is why this type of woman really only takes fairly healthy risks. The self-knowledge that leads her to protect herself from pain means that she will only usually risk a relationship when she knows that it will most probably bring her good things, even if the risk entails the possibility of being left. Now, in the flux of rapidly changing relationships, women are more and more coming to terms with the fact that all relationships will not necessarily lead to life-long partnerships; but they are able to see the benefits of sharing time with a lover who will bring all sorts of gifts to the relationship other than merely the traditional requirement of commitment to marriage. This does, of course, mean that moving in and out of a relationship for a fairly secure woman will cause pain, but hopefully, in the looking back, enough will have been gained to make it seem worth while.

I remember a wonderful, gentle man who literally gave me refuge after I separated from my first husband. During that year, I regained a great deal of confidence in myself. Above all, he opened my eyes to comparative religion in a way that made me understand the beauty of the universal harmony of all things. Even though it was obvious to both of us that our relationship was not permanent, when the time came for him to move in with a woman who offered him a permanent relationship I felt a great deal of pain and loss, but I will be forever grateful for all those good things that he gave me.

I remember that the day he left I lay on my bed and suddenly realised that pain was an old friend. I found myself discussing my symptoms with my 'old friend'. Since then, I have welcomed pain whenever it has been a part of my life. I teach and believe that if you accept pain, as opposed to fighting with it, it can become a creative part of your life. Almost by befriending it, you can come to terms with it. During those weeks after he left, I would deliberately stay away from people so that I didn't distract myself from the necessary mourning for his departure. I cried when I felt like crying, and I treated myself like a treasured invalid, until one day I woke up and saw the sun was shining and I knew the worst was over. Now that risk is a fond memory. I do believe that it is possible to risk yourself if you genuinely do not at the same time delude yourself.

The third category, the disastrous risk-taker is usually a woman who has had a traumatic childhood. Everyone will recognise this type of woman, who seems to stagger from one awful relationship to another. It is perfectly possible for any-one to get into a bad relationship by accident, but the distin-guishing factor between the disastrous risk-taker and everyone else is that she continues to make the same mess time and time again. The first time can be an accident, the second time can be a mistake, the third time careless, but after that there are no excuses. She is a disaster-prone woman and she doesn't need sympathetic friends – she needs treatment. Refuges are full of these women, all claiming they are victims of men's aggres-sions. Unfortunately, they are often encouraged by the vociferous extremes of the Women's Movement, who have merely translated their own failures to work at good relation-ships with men into a political ideology. Sadly, it is precisely these disastrous risk-takers who give a bad name to the women who genuinely need the comfort and security of a safe place.

The hallmark of the habitually disaster-prone woman is the fact that she will return again and again to the relationship that she complains about to all and sundry. This is the woman who will come to the office in such a demoralised state that everyone is soon aware that she has 'problems at home'. Before long she has involved everyone around her. She recounts at great length the awful things that 'he' does. She spends hours on the phone to him. It seems she spends all night fighting and all day making it up.

Well-meaning people involve themselves in advising her, listening to her, getting her shopping, doing her work when she is too distraught to cope. The boss gives her time off. She may come in with the odd bruise, or even really beaten up. Everyone is horrified. She must leave him. Everyone pitches in to help her. But gradually they all realise she isn't going to leave him – not ever. If he leaves her, it won't take her long to find exactly the same sort of man. Everybody is fed up with her, and you can hear the brutal words: 'She asks for it . . .' and 'She likes it . . .' The disastrous risk-taker can give all women a bad name. The fact is, however, that it is totally untrue that any woman likes or enjoys pain, be it emotional or physical. Women who end up in terrible relationships do so because they have experienced similarly painful relationships in early childhood. Behind every man or woman who destroys themselves and others in their pain is a damaged child that needs to be healed. As they go from one desperate situation to another, they become more and more despairing, until finally they often take their own life. It is important for anyone who gets involved with a disastrous risk-taker to get out fast. Too many people think that they can be a therapist to their lover – it doesn't work. Often you feel you can see the hurt child in a terribly damaged human being and you want to mother that child better. Don't fool yourself. If you recognise yourself in this third category, ask for help. Otherwise you will end up old and alone.

When I look back I'm glad I took risks. I feel sorry for the women I know who have been so frightened of life that they deny themselves any part of that wonderful feast to which we are all invited. Certainly, disastrous risk-takers are unhappy women, but I've seen them come to terms with themselves and the echoes of their childhoods, and make real relationships that were created out of choice and not out of neurotic compulsion. I certainly believe that you *have* to have loved and lost before you know how to love at all.

(Originally published February 1982, as 'Love – is it worth the risk?' reprinted by kind permission of *Cosmopolitan* magazine)

IF RAPE IS INEVITABLE

I blocked off this whole near-rape episode in my life. Partly because it was tied up with those three years I was on my own and so insecure about everything that, had I been raped, I'm sure I would have agreed with anyone that cared to tell me that I deserved it. It wasn't until February 1982, when some judge decided to let a rapist off on the grounds that the girl who hitched a lift from him colluded in the act of sex, that I felt so outraged I had to write in defence of women.

It was on a cold, dark, drizzling winter evening three years ago that I booked a mini-cab to take me to a dinner party in Wandsworth. After a hectic hour of feeding the children, the two dogs and the cats, it was a relief to hear a bang on the door – the mini-cab. Shouting last-minute instructions to my children over my shoulder, I left my house. The decision to sit in the front of the cab probably saved my life.

During my three years as a single parent, I used several mini-cab firms when I went out at night, because I knew I drank more than the legal limit of alcohol. Since I always used the same few firms I felt safe with the drivers. My reservations about using just any old firm came from years of experience of working with violent families. I knew that many of the violent men I interviewed often found self-employed jobs such as painting, decorating and driving lorries or taxis – the only way they could earn money, because their violence made them virtually unemployable. Even as I climbed into the front seat, the driver made me very uneasy. He was not one of the regular drivers. He was very big, and as we pulled away from the curb I could see his face set and tense as he accelerated to the lights.

I asked him if he had just joined the firm. He said he had. He was a dangerous and erratic driver. He shouted at other drivers and weaved in and out of the traffic, enjoying the anger and resentment of the other people.

I decided the best way of dealing with the journey was to stay as relaxed as possible and to chat to him. It would be difficult for him to stay in a state of rage if I kept making him laugh. Thank God, I thought, for my years of training. At least we shouldn't have an accident. I knew the house I was going to visit and I also knew the route. It was through Hammersmith, into Fulham Broadway and then to Wandsworth Bridge Road. Across the bridge and then a few roads up was the house. As we approached the bridge, the driver suddenly said he wanted to take a shorter route to avoid the heavy traffic on the bridge. This didn't make sense. There were no other routes across the Thames for several miles. At this point I realised I was in great danger. He turned left down into a road that led to a great waste area of old gasworks and factories. Within minutes we were alone in the car with no houses in sight, only deserted roads, and I could see his hands convulsively gripping the steering-wheel.

I have been aware for years that there are two quite distinct types of rapist. The first, and the most prevalent, are the men who feel that they have a right to rape any woman, who, in their opinion 'asks for it', or 'deserves it'. These men are well protected by society's attitude, particularly the attitude of the court which whole-heartedly agrees with them, if there can be the slightest implication that the woman is in any way less than a respectable pillar of our society.

Henry was a typical example of a marauding male. I knew Henry for several months before I heard that he had attempted to rape a girl I knew, after a party. The profile of rapists usually depicts a man who is unemployed, inadequate and inarticulate. As usual, it allows everyone else to relax, and to think of rape as a working-class problem and, therefore, not worthy of comment unless the matter is dramatically pushed before the public. Then there is a flurry and an outcry, soon to die down as other stories fill the newspapers. However, Henry was a white middle-class insurance-broker, and he was obnoxious. There were three boys in his family. He was adored by his mother because he had been an enchanting-looking child, not very bright but good at games.

His mother would encourage his girlfriends to come home with him, and she would also listen to his boasting of his sexual conquests. She made it quite clear that there were two types of girls: those who did and those who didn't. It was all right to take out those who did, but he was eventually to marry, with his mother's blessing, a nice girl who was still a virgin. That, in a nutshell, was how Henry was conditioned to see women. So when he left home and began to operate as an eligible bachelor he continued to date girls he could write off as 'bad' because they were sexually active. Just how many girls he had raped before he met his match in Caroline, I shall never know.

Middle-class rape, like middle-class violence, goes undetected because everyone involved has too much to lose. The cynical old 'Confucius' saying, 'If rape is inevitable, lie back and enjoy it,' is another way of saying, 'If it happens to you, don't make a fuss.' Thousands and thousands of women hate what happens, but know the price is too high for them to complain.

Henry invited Caroline out to dinner after meeting her at a cocktail party. Henry felt any girl should be obliged to repay his expenses with sexual favours. This time, Caroline asked him back to her flat for coffee. As they sat on the sofa he closed in. Caroline was quite happy to enjoy the sensuous pleasure of kissing but had no intention of having intercourse with a man she had only just met. But Henry was very aroused, and very strong. Before she knew it she was pinned down and he was tearing off her clothes. It was now a question of whether she should scream and wake the neighbours and face public opinion (which is never on the side of a girl living in a flat on her own) or whether she should give in gracefully. Caroline decided to scream. She hollered with such effect that Henry bolted in some disarray.

When I heard about this, I tackled Henry. He was still furious with Caroline. I told him that he deserved to be sent to jail, and indeed it would be appropriate, just as a common thief would face jail. It is no defence in law for a thief to claim that a wallet was protruding from a shopping-bag and therefore was 'asking' to be stolen. The wallet was the property of the owner.

His assertion that Caroline 'asked for it' because she took him back to her flat should not be a mitigating circumstance. Caroline's sexuality was her own legal property, and it was for her only to decide when and if she wanted to have intercourse.

Henry blushed and agreed that I had a point, but there is little chance that he or men like him will behave themselves. Until these sexually rapacious men are brought to heel with a short sharp shock, like a prison sentence, their previous years of conditioning give them a licence to terrorise. In dealing with them, yelling and screaming and what is taught at defence classes are appropriate, because these men *are* responsible for their behaviour. Even during an attempt to force themselves on a woman, they will stop if she can frighten them sufficiently. For them, their goal is their own selfish sexual satisfaction. But they do not intend to kill or to mutilate.

It is the second type of rapist that most concerns me: men like the one in the mini-cab.

I realised, as we drove round and round the dark streets, that this man was not only a rapist but also a possible murderer. His goal was not sexual satisfaction because, quite probably, he would be unable to ejaculate into a woman. His climax would come at the height of a struggle and at the sight of fresh blood. Some of these rapists can only ejaculate after their victim is dead. For others, they can climax at the moment of strangulation when the face of the victim is engorged and the body is convulsing. Usually, these men confine their murderous atacks to prostitutes.

Almost weekly, women and children are found dismembered and mutilated in woods and fields. Often other victims are dumped in the river and never heard of again. The evil underbelly of our increasingly sick society is a law unto itself. A face can disappear from the streets, the word goes round, and no questions are asked. But sometimes the compulsion to kill and to mutilate can overtake the rapist when he has a woman in his power who does not come from his own milieu. Then, unlike the prostitute who faces this kind of man as a daily hazard, she will have no idea of how to save her own life.

The answer, in my eleven years of working with violence; has always been to understand two things. One is that if a violent man feels you are afraid, your fear will escalate his anger and his lust. The second is that any attempt to scream or to struggle will only encite him further. The most important thing you can do is to distract him from his attempts to work himself up to the pitch of rage and excitement that he needs to dissociate himself from reality and to act according to the urgings of his own distorted world. This strange world, unthinkable to normal people, is formed in early childhood. In violent families where everyone behaves violently, the boy-child sees his mother as both a hated and loved enemy who beats him and ill-treats him. Most of these men have promiscuous mothers who are seductive to their sons in between their other relationships with men. The blood-lust seems to come from the boy's witnessing scenes in childhood where, at the height of a beating, the mother is covered in blood. Instead of expressing horror and compassion, these children will describe the blood with a sense of sexual excitement. They will also describe watching their mothers copulating with a similar sense of pleasure. By the time they are in their teens, they are already violent and perverted. These boys, full of conflicting rage and hatred for all women, are dangerous predators, and their goal is deathly. All self-defence classes, and the people who run rape crisis centres, must make a distinction between the two types of rapist. This second type of rapist should not be jailed. He must go to a hospital for the criminally insane, and there be treated. Otherwise, locked up and untreated, he will only compulsively rape again when he is freed.

Using a technique that I learned from years of door-step confrontations with violent men, I went into 'overdrive'. That means I switched off my human feelings and dealt with the mini-cab driver as if he was a patient. First of all I talked enthusiastically about his car, and I made a point of touching his arm in a friendly, confident way. Had I been sitting in the back I would have been unable to hold his attention. I anchored his reality with mine. I asked him if he had brothers and sisters. He answered my friendly, interested voice. I lowered the pitch of my voice until it was gentle and caring. I talked about God. I asked him if he believed in God. He did. These men do what they do, but they still hate themselves. I could see as we talked that his body had begun to relax. His hands loosened on the steering-wheel. I kept my sentences really short, so that he had to think of my words to keep up with the conversation. That way he hadn't the time to slip off into his other world. I don't know at exactly what point he decided to let me go. Probably it was when I talked to him about religion, or maybe it was when I sang 'Ba Ba, Black Sheep' to him as I told him about my grand-daughter's demands that I sing it every night. It was probably then, because he joined in at the end.

What I was doing was reinforcing his concept of women as saints and therefore untouchable, rather than allowing him to slip into his reality where I was a sexual woman, and therefore erotic and dangerous and deserving of death. As we rounded another corner I saw the lights of the bridge and knew I was probably safe. I kept chatting away until we drew up at the door of the house. I paid him off and knocked at the door. When I got inside I allowed my human side to take over. I told my hosts what had happened. They didn't really understand, so I was agitated all evening till I got home to the comfort of my family. I realised that it was probably only my years of dealing with violent people that had saved me from a savage rape attack, or even death. I was powerless to do anything about the man, because you can't touch him in law until he has actually raped someone. (I would like to see all mini-cabs licensed, with much greater attention paid by firms who take on drivers. Otherwise a mini-cab can become a coffin on wheels. Of course most mini-cab drivers aren't like that, and they would probably be more than willing to help weed out any potential rapists in their ranks.)

I was amazed, when I recounted this episode to other women, at how many women had had similar experiences. Often the drivers were just out to rape, and could be talked out of it. But a few women I talked to did give in because they were driven off into blind alleys or unknown areas and decided that it wasn't worth risking their lives. I have never come across a woman who said she enjoyed what happened to her, although I'll be the first to admit that there are women who, like these men, get their pleasure out of pain. These are the women who share the same violent family backgrounds. But we cannot allow the present confused state of affairs to continue, where on one hand we say that all women must have the right to be protected from rapists, and rape should be considered a heinous crime second only to murder and incest, but then, on the other hand, the courts spend much time deciding according to a scale of moral judgement just how innocent the victim has been.

It is probably worth looking back at history to see how our attitudes have been shaped by myths and legends. An excellent source book on this subject is *Women, Androgynes, and Other Mystical Beasts*, written by Wendy O'Flaherty. Men's attitudes are deeply embedded in the ancient archetypal images of women as either nurturers or destroyers. The first image is that of the earth-mother goddess. She is seen as a cow-like submissive creature, subservient to man – her acknowledged master. Her breasts are for feeding purposes alone. Her image is asexual, non-erotic, and because she is a mother figure she is deserving of honour and protection by men. She is epitomised in the cult of the Virgin Mary. The second image is sometimes known as the 'goddess of the tooth'. Here a woman is described in ancient Hindu tradition as a mare, a female horse out of control, her huge teeth and bulging eyes bearing down on the defenceless male. She is castrating, demonic and erotic. She is perceived as dark and evil and deserves to be conquered by an act of rape, multilated and killed.

Because there are women who encourage acts of sexual violence for their own sick needs, we must not let them be used as an excuse to brand all women with the label of provocation. Women and men should all work together towards re-educating the courts to a realistic perception of what *actually* occurred in a particular incident of sexual violence towards a woman. Otherwise rape is left to hysterical press-reporting and blind prejudice. It does not further the course of justice to have small groups of women taking advantage of a rape to declare their hatred of men by proclaiming that all men are rapists or are violent. Most men are neither, and are bitterly ashamed of the violent members of their own sex. They are only too willing to help find solutions.

If we do not accept an uncompromising attitude towards violent people, the streets will not be a safe place for ourselves and our children. A nation that does not rigorously protect its members who are vulnerable to attack is corrupt and decadent. At present we have the most powerful roles in this country in the hands of women. The Queen is the reigning monarch and she is also the head of the Church. The Prime Minister is also a woman, and it is fitting that the subject of violence towards women should be tackled as a matter of urgency.

(Originally published July 1982, as 'Living in a dangerous age', reprinted by kind permission of *Cosmopolitan* magazine)

FOR WHOM THE BELL TOLLS

It was Pat Garratt, my editor, who sent me an American article about the moaning male and asked me if I felt I could elaborate on the subject. I must say I was amazed at the very deep and sore views it exposed. I even apologised at the end of the piece in case all men would cross the road when they saw me pass by.

Women have always administered to lepers. When a man is not a physical leper, but an emotional leper, then women get badly hurt – the physical and emotional diseases are both catching. One day the ministering angel wakes up to find herself filled with loathing and self-disgust, while her partner steps over her prostrate body and, ringing his little leper's bell, sails forth again looking for an unsuspecting victim. The problem with this sort of man is that he comes in such a variety of disguises that it is almost impossible to spot him.

I think the most classic symptom is that he tends to look like a small lost boy loitering on the corner of life. The first instinct he arouses is compassion. How could anyone pass by such a bewildered helpless child? Be he a managing director or the local plumber, he knows the routine so well that he has most of it down pat. His first commitment is to himself. That might sound obvious, but it takes a woman time to realise that he is not aware of the possibility that there is such a thing as commitment to anyone else. Most of us recognise that the world could be described as a stage with all of us taking part in a huge play. This type of man, however, has only one actor on the stage – himself. All other parts are merely walk-on parts, including the lady in his life at that moment.

I watched Jane, a girlfriend of mine, nearly die from the infection of her partner Philip. They had lived together for two years, after meeting at a party where Philip seemed to be the only intelligent, sensitive man among a crowd of rather chauvinistic males. He talked perceptively to Jane about his feelings of sexism, and Jane, who was always a bit naïve when it came to men, fell head-over-heels in love with him. I was a bit wary when she told me that he hated phoning women, so she would have to get in touch with him. I put that down to my bourgeois conditioning and refrained from comment. However, Jane invited him over to her flat for dinner and they had a wonderful evening discussing all his old relationships with other women. He left saying that he couldn't possibly sleep with her because he had hurt so many women he didn't want to feel guilty about his relationship with her. Jane felt it was all very noble. I felt it was all very suspect.

The next scene for Jane was at his flat, with two of his ex-lovers. The wretched man had an amazing ability to retain the affection of most of the women he had very nearly destroyed. Dinner consisted of Philip talking over all his problems with the three attentive women. I would have been bored out of my bracket because, as a counsellor, I have listened to many women repeating their men's same parrot-like dialogue. He says he is so dreadful, so unworthy, so corrupt that he feels he is not fit to tie her shoe-laces. What the woman doesn't realise is that all the while he is confessing, he is tying her shoe-laces together, so that when he is bored and all set to run off, she gets up to follow him and falls flat on her face.

It took two and a half years for Philip to almost totally destroy Jane – who, with her small-town upbringing which made her less cynical than her London contemporaries, had a sweet and ebullient nature. Gradually she got thinner and paler, and then her shoulders hunched over from the pain. She semed always preoccupied, as though trying to sort out a puzzle of such mystifying proportions that it really took up all her energies. She seemed to walk in a dream. The puzzle was the confused messages of love and rejection that she constantly received from Philip.

Men like Philip are from a generation that took self-analysis to their masculine bosoms like there was no tomorrow. They realised in the Sixties that a sure way to a woman's heart was through her psyche. Women, having felt isolated for centuries from communicating with men (who, on the whole, preferred to communicate with each other), fell head over heels for this ploy. At last women believed they had found a soul-mate – a man who could relate to them and share all the deep wonder in the true union between that which is male and that which is female. Certainly there are those men around, but their hallmark is their reticence.

Emotionally leprous men ooze like pus the psychobabble learned from the knee of their most recent analysts. Usually they choose a woman analyst, so that they can mine nuggets of information that can later be used to undermine another female. 'My analyst says . . .' and as she is a woman, it makes her comments sound more valid. However, should the woman analyst make any attempt to blow his game, all she will have is an empty couch and an overdraft. It won't take him long to find a fatherly male analyst who will collude in his version of himself.

Of course the primary aim of men like Philip is to put a woman in a position where she takes the responsibility for everything that occurs. He makes it his business to be hauled struggling and protesting through any event in their lives. This way, whatever goes wrong, it's all her fault. Then, instead of berating her, he is quite likely to make the game more complicated by berating himself. This way, he elicits a double helping of her guilt. She is guilty for herself and guilty that he feels guilty.

A typical set-up occurs when the phone rings and someone asks the couple to a party. He can begin this game by pointing out that he hates parties: 'Can't think of anything to say. Nobody ever talks to me.' She is so busy coaxing him, she doesn't notice that he is already finding himself a clean shirt and has every intention of going. When they get there, he has a marvellous time in a corner with a girl with the biggest knockers in England. In no time he is discussing his fear of breasts as a primary betrayal in his childhood, and the girl is getting so sympathetic she is about to offer herself to him. At this point he mentions his girlfriend, leaving a bewildered woman sitting in a corner wondering why she is feeling so confused. She is confused because these men are so clever at catching a woman and luring her into a deep and feeling pool. The woman doesn't realise that he has no deep end at all, only the shallowest of shallows. She responds to his manipulations and gives all she has, only to find that when he is bored with the conversation he will throw it all back in her face. That sort of 'conversation interruptus' over a number of years can emotionally destroy a woman. She does all the giving, and he does all the living.

Take Mark and the subject of marriage. I personally do not care to share the same air as Mark. I have an overwhelming desire to shove his head through a plate-glass window. Such is the damage he has done to at least four women, to my knowledge. Mark makes it absolutely clear to any woman he comes across that he is the most unmarriageable prospect she has ever encountered. Facts speak for themselves, because he has been divorced three times. A quick guided tour through his awful childhood (details change from one story to another) and he usually has a woman hooked after the first hour. There he sits, head on one side, nervously brushing his hair from his eyes with his heavily nicotine-stained fingers. He has perfected the act of fluttering his eyelashes and peering up shyly at his listener to such a degree it would make a geisha spit.

By this time it is useless to warn the already hooked lady. I know – I've tried. Yet again, he sets up a relationship with a woman in which he draws up all the ground rules: (1) No commitment; (2) Always openness and honesty about other affairs; (3) No marriage; (4) No questions asked. Conclusion of contract is that both sides are totally free. Their love will bypass all problems, particularly the problem that Mark is an unutterable, dedicated shit. Like in potty-training, some women seem just as dedicated to clearing up after him. The first year was always the best in Mark's affairs. He liked to play at 'being in love', arriving with flowers, remembering anniversaries, and buying records. Romance laid on with a trowel. In this unromantic age, it leaves most women breathless. The first year passes in a whirl, but the rows get bigger as the months go by.

It seems to women trying to care for the Marks and Philips of this world that, all the while they are holding his hand and propping up his rapidly receding self-esteem, they have become screaming viragos. Friends of mine who normally consider themselves self-controlled professional women can be heard from the street outside. As their voices get higher and louder, his voice gets more and more calm, more and more reasonable. 'I drive you to this,' he says clutching his head. 'It's all my fault; you deserve better than me.' The hurt look in his eye and the slight tremble of his otherwise manly lips precipitate her into his arms again.

'Don't worry, darling,' she whispers as they make for the bed. He isn't worried; he's just randy. When he's finished, she rolls over and buries her head in the pillow, and wonders why she is crying. She asks herself, like so many other women, 'Is this all there is in a relationship between a man and a woman?' Of course it isn't, but for many women, trained by their mothers to expect very little for themselves, that is all they ask for. 'Any man is better than no man' is still preached as regularly as a Sunday sermon. I only have to listen to the conversations in the ladies' changing rooms at the Hogarth Health Club to realise that little has changed. True, there are now many women who have made a promise to themselves that they would rather be alone than put up with a second-rate relationship, like those offered by such leprous men, but they pay a very high price for it. They are shunned not only by many men, who see a woman on her own as a threat to be either conquered or ignored, but also, more tragically, by other women who want them around for solace and comfort, but underneath it all see them as another sort of threat – to their possession of their own men.

Many women of my age who either have refused to compromise themselves by getting into a makeshift marriage, or have bailed themselves out of a leaking one, now face an uncertain middle age. But they do so with far more confidence than their mothers and grandmothers.

Getting away from a man like Mark takes a formidable amount of character. For while he insists on the one hand that marriage is the last thing he would ever contemplate, he slowly but surely edges a woman into a corner where she feels that maybe the only thing that will save him from himself is for her to make the supreme sacrifice of her dignity and self-respect, so she offers to marry him. Yet again, she is in a position where she has taken the sole responsibility for what should be a shared commitment. 'Oh, very well – if that's what you want,' is usually the reluctant acceptance to the proposal, wrenched from his unwilling lips. 'Don't say I didn't warn you. You know what I'm like.'

Mark did marry my friend Rachel – it was his fourth time. Last I saw of her, she was a wreck. Mark was sweetly reasonable, and everyone was talking about how difficult his new wife was.

Living with a man whose strategies are designed to keep a woman in the full-time occupation of inflating his ego is like becoming an Axminster carpet while he like a Hoover sucks the life out of her and emotionally beats as he sweeps and cleans. Those women who do get out, with much help from friends who have been similarly afflicted, face the incredulity of their nearest and dearest, to say nothing of their neighbours! 'He was such a nice man, so kind, so considerate. He understood women.' He certainly did. If he spent as much time earning money as he spent making a woman suffer, at least she could suffer in wealth. Part of his failure syndrome is his ability to be terribly good at something for a very short time, and then it's all downhill from there. Being good at something is dangerous for his long-term plans of making everything everybody else's fault. But the most exasperating part of this whole conundrum is that such men bring out the mentor in women. We are all trained to elicit talent from our men. The leprous male withholds all his gifts, and the woman tries desperately to make him realise his full potential. The woman usually ends up burned out for her efforts, as the man moves on to lure the sympathies of other unsuspecting females.

Before a huge section of male readers overdose in despair, I would like to make it clear that I do not include the majority of men in this category, and that women have similar problems of their own and can be equally dangerous, only they use different strategies. Still, there are sufficient amount of leprous men around for me to remind other women that leprosy is a notifiable disease. Please leave it to a fully qualified SRN.

(Originally published November 1982, as 'Are you a sucker for the little boy lost?', reprinted by kind permission of *Cosmopolitan* magazine)

THE JUDAS SYNDROME

Yet again somebody very closely connected with my work had turned out to have been selling me short for years. The great pleasure in writing it all down is very cathartic. Another pleasure is the knowledge that they may recognise themselves in print and, hopefully, so will their friends.

I suddenly realised the other day, as I cast yet another weary eye over my misspent youth, that I seemed to have surrounded myself with a fair number of people who, under the guise of friendship, turned out to be people who were anything but friendly after the initial honeymoon period was over. I subsequently thought about the role of treachery and betrayal, and decided that in future I would be far more wary of professed friendships, as I have a tendency, from an early unloved childhood, to be immensely grateful to anyone who shows an interest in me or my work. Instead of counting the stab-wounds and wallowing in self-pity, I decided to try to understand what makes a traitor.

The problem for the betrayer is always that in the end they finally betray themselves. Those people who are not, by nature, betrayers often find the motives of a betrayer very puzzling. Take the classic example of the office betrayer. Sally is an extremely good shorthand-typist. She looks neat and competent and is very hard-working. The men and women on the floor of the advertising agency were delighted when she joined them. It didn't take long for them to bitterly regret their decision. After the first month, Sally knew just about everything that happened on that floor. Because she seemed so concerned and loving, everyone poured out their heart and soul into her tiny manipulative hands. Once firmly established as a capable secretary, she was promoted to work for the boss. Power at last.

Now, with the boss more than willing to let her take over the more boring parts of his job, she became so efficient that she rendered him almost redundant, and very dependent on her. However, the most emotionally satisfying part of the job for her lay in manipulating the staff. 'He's in a bad mood,' she would say, leaving the boss's office and closing the door. That was quite enough to keep people away, so she effectively isolated the boss from his workforce. Soon, if anyone annoyed her, she would hint to a senior member of staff, 'Maybe you'd better check Maureen. She seems to be using the phone rather a lot.' She operated by creating fear and paranoia. Those who obeyed her were rewarded, and those that refused to gossip and connive with her were ruthlessly punished. Allegations about their honesty, their personal habits and their relationships would pour from her lips in a venomous torrent. But so cleverly concealed was the poison that it sounded like tender concern.

For all betrayers, it is the rule that behind any allegation there lies a grain of truth which can then be polished, embellished and distorted to the satisfaction of the betrayer and to the detriment of the betrayed. When finally the office as a whole had had enough and they combined to get rid of her, it was her finest hour as she fought back with all the skill and acid accusations she could muster. The rest of the staff, exhausted and white-faced with all the catastrophe and hurt feelings, limped home, but she bounced back ready for the fray day after day. At last she met her match and was sacked. At this point an office betrayer like Sally can either move on and cause havoc again somewhere else, or face herself and learn something about her own needs.

Any of the potentially parasite professions are classic positions for betrayers. For workers in these professions, such as lawyers, accountants, or agents, act as a mediator between two interested parties. Obviously many people pursuing these professions do so out of a healthy and authentic sense of service. However, these roles offer ideal opportunities for betrayal for anyone so inclined, and the damage they can wreak is vast and pernicious. That is why these professions are so hated by often confused men and women who have appointed a professional third party to look after their interests, only to find that the mediator has skipped off with most of the money, having acted against the clients' best interest.

In a way, women tend to betray through internal personal relationships. The maxim that 'the hand that rocks the cradle rules the world' is drummed into little girls from birth. They manipulate far more subtly than men. They practise a multi-layer duplicity that usually can only be detected by other women. Men tend to be far more obvious though I've known some expert operators in the past – like Ralph. Ralph practises matrimonial law. His is a very established practice. He is ambitious and determined to succeed. Unfortunately, the senior partner who hired him did not realise that his success would be at everyone else's expense.

Normal people get their rewards and satisfaction from a job well and nobly done; a betrayer get his or her satisfaction from the moment he or she has managed to hurt and bewilder another human being. Matrimonial law is ideal for a ruthless lawyer to play endless games between already dissenting couples. The game is doubly exciting, because not only is there the satisfaction of inflicting pain on an already painful situa-tion, but there is also an escalating financial reward while bleeding dry the supposedly cared-for client. A supreme moment for Ralph would come when he had made deals behind some desperate woman's back. Then, on the appointed day when the couple meet in the divorce courts, she finds herself with less money, unsatisfactory custody arrangements, and a huge bill. Supporting her sobbing form, her caring solicitor will lead her from the court, saying he is as puzzled as she is as to why, after all his optimistic words, they fared so badly. Later, when she has had time to think, she will grow furious as she realises that he betrayed her. Too late, I am afraid. The more treacherous the profession, the more securely it guards its members, so complaining never gets anyone very far.

The ultimate betrayal is when the betrayer turns traitor to his or her country. Men are far more likely to betray their country than women. I often wonder if this is because England is seen as the 'motherland', and thus female, while communism has a very patriarchal image. Mother-damaged men can escalate the game to where they betray personally, nationally, and then internationally.

In relationships, the betrayal game can be deadly. If, by chance, two betrayers get together, the situation can end in one killing the other. However, it doesn't often happen this way, because a betrayer is much more inclined to look for an unsuspecting victim. There is more room for destruction that way. In all my time at the Refuge, I have been amazed at the number of women victims who have come to me from all walks of life, whether their partners were national figures or unemployed. It was not the ill-treatment, both physical and mental that drove them into my care; it was the fact that their partners had been unfaithful. It was not even the sex with the other women that hurt them so badly. It was the pain of betrayal that wounded them so deeply that some were never able to recover from it.

Most of us, hopefully, were born into warm, loving families. Some of us were not. Those of us who weren't could be said to have been 'emotionally disabled' by that experience. It is every child's birthright to be a wanted, loved child, but unfortunately the world is not a perfect place. If children are born physically disabled we now, as a society, make efforts to protect and care for them, instead of leaving them out to die, as was the practice centuries ago. But, unfortunately, for those who start life emotionally disadvantaged, there is very little such provision.

Babies born into warm, loving families learn to relax and to enjoy their parenting. If they are hurt or upset, the parents are there to comfort and to care. These children grow up to continue to make warm loving relationships in the outside world. Even if life delivers a couple of foul blows, they have enough inner resources and sufficient good relationships to get up, dust themselves down, and begin all over again.

Babies born into emotionally disabled families virtually have to learn strategies for their own survival from birth onwards. Depending on the type of damage experienced within the family, these children will develop techniques to enable them to sustain their own lives within that circle. The pattern that makes betrayers develops when such a child learns to play one parent off against the other.

James was born into a professional family, and until the birth of twin sisters seven years later, he enjoyed the luxury of being an only child. The father was a cold silent man with an academic mind, who kept himsef away from most of the family rows. The purveyor of the drama in this family was the mother. Thrilled with the birth of James, she decided that he would grow up to be the leading musician of his day. She hardly ever put him down. When she was not creating dramas with her husband, she was squeezing and fondling James. Her husband retreated further and further into the background, until James was seven.

Then, suddenly, James noticed his mother was pregnant. Now James was at an age when he had picked up all sorts of information about sex. His mother had been obsessed with James to such an extent that he had virtually been encouraged to sleep in his parents' bed until he was of school age; then his father put his foot down. When James realised that she had done 'those disgusting things' with his father, James was overwhemed by a searing pain of betrayal.

Once the twins were born, even James's mother was too tired to throw tantrums. James was no longer the centre of her universe. The pain of that early betrayal remained with him all his life.

In a loving family where the child shares in his parents' relationship, by about the age of three the child makes the momentous step forward from only perceiving himself in the universe, to being able to experience other people sharing that space. The betrayed child, however, never makes that step. By the time the child should be turning outwards, he will have learned that the world is too dangerous a place. He will lower the portcullis in his soul and begin to build a fortress.

In James's case, his emotionally incestuous mother – who not only first seduced him for his own bad needs, but also encouraged him to betray his father by adopting her own dismissive attitude to his fatherly role in the family – left him doubly bereft. It was too late to turn to a father who, by the time the sisters arrived, felt deeply resentful of his son's place in his wife's affections. James fought back with all the hurt and rage he could express. He manipulated situations and created fights whenever he could. Even at seven he held the family to ransom. They retaliated by sending him away to boarding-school – a further betrayal. Never again would a child like James trust another woman.

Exactly the same can be said of the attitude towards men held by a *girl* born into a family where the parents are disenchanted with each other, and where the father turns to the girl-child for solace and comfort. She too will learn strategies to keep his attention for herself and away from the mother. Eventually, the child will feel the betrayal of a man who should have been a father but acted more like a lover. Because she will have had to develop the techniques of flirtatious behaviour so young, she will never know the innocence which is the true hallmark of childhood.

This, then, is how betrayers are created. Filled with hatred instead of love, the pain of the original betrayal lies deep inside them. They are driven to acting out their rage at other people's expense. Some people from betrayed backgrounds pursue careers that bring them in the public eye, becoming powerful figures – politicians or performers. In fact, many of our greatest operas, plays and works of literature are about the theme of betrayal. If they can come to terms with their original betrayal, then such people can act and entertain out of true creativity. Otherwise, they create only out of their own damage, and their careers will often have an ignominious end.

Whatever profession the betrayer chooses, he or she will spend much of their physical and emotional lives trying to create frenzied events to stay away from the original primary pain. Jeff and I call this effort to distract and to create diversions 'secondary pain'. By this we mean that such persons will usually fill their lives (and the lives of those unsuspecting people who are involved with them) with urgent, chaotic, painful events. In repeated dreadful relationships, the betrayers will manipulate until the events overtake them and once again they are out on their own and in pain. Office rows and dramas fed Sally's bad needs (as we saw at the beginning of the article) as she paid everyone back for her original hurt. James is still going back to his mother, whom he both loves and hates. Unable to deal with the pain of her betrayal, he destroys all women under the guise of practising a selfless legal vocation for the rights of women.

These people are terribly dangerous both to themselves and to anyone in their path. It is easy to dislike them once they have been exposed, but it is only an understanding of their own condition that makes it possible for them to seek help and to learn to trust human beings again. This requires an arduous journey into the past, and that is dreadfully painful. But the danger is that totally unwitting people, or even a chance event, can also throw a person suffering from this pain back into their past. Once the secondary pain is in touch with the primary pain, the two resonate. For many people it is so unbearable that they kill themselves. Many people who commit suicide do so for this reason.

It takes great skill and care, and much trust, to accept a destructive person's need to create hurt and damage, and to gently follow them along the road into the mists of childhood, back to the original source of pain. Once the memories of that betrayal are poured out and shared, the relief is enormous. The pain slowly fades away and the person is literally newborn.

Many women who have come to us in the Refuge have had several unhappy and treacherous relationships. They are hurt and distraught because they truly loved their men. In some cases where the couple were able to understand why the man behaved the way he did (or in some cases, where the woman was a betrayer, the man had to understand why she did the things she did) there was sufficient love between them to heal each other. Sometimes it is an impossible task: the one partner has decided to play Judas for life. In that case the only kiss you can allow is when you say goodbye.

(Originally published August 1982, as 'Whodunnit? Erin Pizzey detects treachery', reprinted by kind permission of *Cosmopolitan* magazine)

FAREWELL, SHEPHERD'S BUSH

I end with this piece because I'm off adventuring again. No doubt the Great American Adventure will be another book. So, with love to everyone, I'm off, and for those of you who are interested in writing yourselves, take advice from me: don't talk about it, start scribbling.

The 'For Sale' sign is outside the front door. It hurts to sell something you love so much. This house was designed as a dower house for the local manor, so it housed the mother-in-law. It is a very matronly house, and I fell in love with it as soon as I saw it. I've been here eleven years – the longest I've been anywhere in my life. I started Women's Aid here, and here I wrote three books. I got divorced here. I shared the house with my ex-husband for the children's sake. I spent three gruelling years learning about loneliness and had a nervous breakdown. I fell rapturously in love with Jeff, who fell out of a van at my feet. I was married from here.

My father died last Christmas, and in spite of his dreadful relationship with my mother and the loving care of his third wife, he asked that his ashes be scattered on my mother's grave. The day we were to scatter the ashes, my new mother-in-law charged through the front door uninvited from Boston and said she wouldn't leave till the police were called.

'You've been divorced, you have illegitimate half-caste grandchildren, you've had a nervous breakdown, and,' she said, working herself up to a climax, 'your father's dead.' Put like that, I didn't seem much of a proposition. Finally, as Jeff put her firmly in a taxi for the airport, she was heard to howl: 'You're stealing a twenty-year-old boy!'

The neighbours will miss all the drama – as when the National Front stood ouside the door shouting, 'Erin Pizzey, out, out, out.' They ran off when I opened the door. I can't say I blame them.

Most of all I'll miss the garden. Surprisingly, for such a restless soul as myself, I actually *believed* Jeff when he said not everything I touched would die. We grew all sorts of beautiful plants together. Last year we had potatoes, carrots, tomatoes and boxes of herbs. Every day was warm. I cooked huge meals and we lay out with half of Shepherd's Bush dropping by to play ping-pong. I'll miss half of Shepherd's Bush. Everywhere I go, they turn up.

This house has raised my own children and my grandchildren. This house has also protected many vulnerable, battered children. As my private refuge, it has acted as a deterrent to parents who would lash out, except for the fact that there was another place to go for the cowering child. It's a shabby house, because I have never had much money to spend on it. Like many women, I took no maintenance after my divorce, relying on my belief in God that I could write for a living. This was an act of faith, just as leaving for America with only the money left over from the sale of this house and a belief that our new book together (*Prone to Violence*, October 1982) will change people's thinking is an act of faith.

The world is such a beautiful place. It is like a huge banquet and we are all invited guests. Unfortunately, we are mostly trained to stay in the kitchen. We all have things to do and places to go, but, for most of us, we dream all our hopes away. I have realised that our life's work will be explaining to the emotionally able community what it is like being emotionally disabled. If someone has no legs, you get them a wheelchair. If life's circumstances so cripple another human being that they are emotionally disabled, we tend to punish them. We can write such books anywhere – so the family consulted together and we decided to look for a place in the sun. We would have to live very cheaply, grow our own food, and take the huge risk that all writers take. If we can't sell our books, there is nowhere to go back to. If we can't make a living by writing, then both of us will have to get a job locally, or we hope we could always open a restaurant. Most people have lots of options but they never explore them.

My ex-husband helped the decision, because he too decided to spread his wings and, with his new wife, is now in Australia making excellent documentaries. 1982 is a time to venture forth. England is a small island with a magical force that attracts people from all over the world. We have the best of everything here: music, opera, drama, food, fashion. The well of original creative thought lies somewhere here on this island. You have only to stand in our cathedrals and see the soaring arches rise like frozen music to feel that we are close to God. I will miss that spine-tingling feeling of being near so many creative and inspired people. But we have always exported our talent to other countries. I have had English teas in such faraway places as Singapore, Penang and New Zealand. I will no doubt take my Englishness with me. It has taken Jeff two years to sort out his 'tomatoes', and 'pyjamas', to say nothing of 'aluminium'. Now we go into reverse. I think I'll stay English.

I suppose my dream is that by this time next year we will have done it. We have to go in two lots, which is probably just as well for the American customs officials. We have to leave my daughter Cleo and the grandchildren behind for three months, because I have to be already over there to apply to get her in. The heartlessness of bureaucratic immigration laws bewilders me. Jeff, Amos, China (the Pekingese) and myself leave first, heading for the boat with our American camper piled high with all our worldly goods. We will drive to New Mexico and look for somewhere to live. Then we will send for Cleo, the two grandchildren, and two Shepherd's Bush moggies known as Boy-cat and Girl-cat. Quite how they will cope away from Shepherd's Bush, I know not. But they have been with me all their lives and no one else could put up with their eccentric ways. Anyway they are fully part of the family, as is China.

What will the Americans make of us? Will New Mexico get used to Amos' dreadlocks? Will I cope with an American life-style? Will they cope with mine – a 43-year-old, middle-aged hippy? I hope so. That's why it's all so exciting. I feel the joy of realising I can live internationally. I can be as much here as I can there. I can keep my finger on both pulses. I can communicate between two continents. Once I become detached from the pain of losing my possessions, I can soar. Who knows? After New Mexico, it might be Alaska, China, or even Tibet. I *do* believe that the world *is* a banquet, and my family are all sitting at the table with our napkins under our chins.

(Originally pubished May 1982, as 'Why I'm getting up and going', reprinted by kind permission of *Cosmopolitan* magazine)

NON-FICTION

GENERAL

☐ The Chinese Mafia	Fenton Bresler	£1.50
☐ Here Comes Everybody	Anthony Burgess	£1.75
☐ Basil Ede's Birds	Dougall & Ede	£4.95
☐ Strange Deaths	John Dunning	£1.50
☐ Truly Murderous	John Dunning	£1.50
☐ Ielfstan's Place	Richard Girling	£1.95

TRAVEL

☐ The Complete Traveller	Joan Bakewell	£1.95
☐ Camping in Comfort	Dymphna Byrne	£1.75
☐ A Walk Around the Lakes	Hunter Davies	£1.95
☐ Weekend Cycling	Christa Gausden	£1.95
☐ Britain by Train	Patrick Goldring	£1.75
☐ England by Bus	Elizabeth Gundrey	£1.75
☐ Staying Off the Beaten Track *(revised edition)*	Elizabeth Gundrey	£2.95
☐ Weekend Walking	Roger Smith	£1.95
☐ Britain at Your Feet	Wickers & Pedersen	£1.75

BIOGRAPHY/AUTOBIOGRAPHY

☐ All You Needed Was Love	John Blake	£1.50
☐ The Queen Mother Herself	Helen Cathcart	£1.25
☐ Clues to the Unknown	Robert Cracknell	£1.50
☐ George Stephenson	Hunter Davies	£1.50
☐ William Wordsworth	Hunter Davies	£2.50
☐ The Family Story	Lord Denning	£1.95
☐ Nelson	Harry Edgington	£1.50
☐ The Admiral's Daughter	Victoria Fyodorova	£1.75
☐ Nancy Astor	John Grigg	£2.95
☐ Monty	Nigel Hamilton	£4.95
☐ Fifty Years with Mountbatten	Charles Smith	£1.25
☐ Maria Callas	Arianna Stassinopoulos	£1.75
☐ Swanson on Swanson	Gloria Swanson	£2.95

REFERENCE

☐ The Sunday Times Guide to Movies on Television	Angela & Elkan Allan	£1.50
☐ Hunter Davies's Book of British Lists		£1.25
☐ Hunter Davies's Bigger Book of British Lists		£1.50
☐ NME Guide to Rock Cinema	Fred Dellar	£1.50
☐ The Book of Beasts	John May & Michael Marten	£4.95
☐ The Drinker's Companion	Derek Nimmo	£1.25
☐ Money Matters	Raymond Painter	£1.50
☐ The Complete Book of Cleaning	Barty Phillips	£1.50
☐ The Oscar Movies from A–Z *(revised)*	Roy Pickard	£1.75
☐ Islam	D. S. Roberts	£1.50
☐ Questions of Motoring Law	John Spencer	£1.25
☐ Questions of Law	Bill Thomas	£1.50
☐ Questions of Law: Homes	Trevor M. Aldridge	£1.50

WAR

☐ The Battle of Malta	Joseph Attard	£1.50
☐ The Shape of Wars to Come	David Baker	£3.95
☐ World War 3	Shelford Bidwell (ed.)	£1.75
☐ The Black Angels	Rupert Butler	£1.50
☐ Gestapo	Rupert Butler	£1.50
☐ Hand of Steel	Rupert Butler	£1.35
☐ The Air Battle for Malta	Lord James Douglas-Hamilton	£1.50
☐ The Flight of the Mew Gull	Alex Henshaw	£1.75
☐ Sigh for a Merlin	Alex Henshaw	£1.50
☐ Hitler's Secret Life	Glenn B. Infield	£1.50
☐ The War Machine	James Avery Joyce	£1.50
☐ Spitfire into Battle	Group Captain Duncan Smith	£1.75

NON-FICTION

HEALTH/SELF-HELP

☐	The Hamlyn Family First Aid Book	Dr Robert Andrew	£1.50
☐	Girl!	Brandenburger & Curry	£1.25
☐	Eat Yourself Slim	Rosemary Conley	£1.25
☐	The Good Health Guide for Women	Cooke & Dworkin	£2.95
☐	The Babysitter Book	Cunningham & Curry	£1.25
☐	Enjoying Retirement	Jennifer Curry	£1.50
☐	Pulling Your Own Strings	Dr Wayne W. Dyer	£1.50
☐	Living Together	Dyer & Berlins	£1.50
☐	Clever Children	Dr Joan Freeman	£1.50
☐	Coping with Redundancy	Kemp, Buttle & Kemp	£1.50
☐	Cystitis: A Complete Self-help Guide	Angela Kilmartin	£1.00
☐	Fit for Life	Donald Norfolk	£1.50
☐	The Stress Factor	Donald Norfolk	£1.25
☐	Fat is a Feminist Issue	Susie Orbach	£1.25
☐	Fat is a Feminist Issue II *(Cassette and Booklet)*	Susie Orbach	£3.50
☐	Prone to Violence	Erin Pizzey and Jeff Shapiro	£1.75
☐	Living With Your New Baby	Rakowitz & Rubin	£1.50
☐	Sexual Harassment at Work	Sue Read	£1.50
☐	Natural Sex	Mary Shivanandan	£1.25
☐	A–Z of Family Medicines	Rosalind Spencer	£1.75
☐	Health Shock	Martin Weitz	£1.75

POCKET HEALTH GUIDES

☐	Migraine	Dr Finlay Campbell	65p
☐	Pre-menstrual Tension	June Clark	65p
☐	Back Pain	Dr Paul Dudley	65p
☐	Allergies	Robert Eagle	65p
☐	Asthma	Robert Eagle	85p
☐	Arthritis & Rheumatism	Dr Luke Fernandes	65p
☐	Cystitis	Diane Fernyhough	85p
☐	Circulation Problems	J. A. Gillespie	85p
☐	Depression and Anxiety	Dr Arthur Graham	85p
☐	Anaemia	Dr Alexander D. G. Gunn	85p
☐	Diabetes	Dr Alexander D. G. Gunn	85p
☐	Heart Trouble	Dr Simon Joseph	85p
☐	High Blood Pressure	Dr James Knapton	85p
☐	Peptic Ulcers	Drs Martin & Stiel	85p
☐	Hysterectomy	Wendy Savage	85p
☐	The Menopause	Studd & Thom	85p
☐	Skin Troubles	Deanna Wilson	65p
☐	Children's Illnesses	Dr Luke Zander	85p

COOKERY

☐	A to Z of Health Foods	Carol Bowen	£1.50
☐	The Giant Sandwich Book	Carol Bowen	£1.25
☐	Vegetarian Cookbook	Dave Dutton	£1.50
☐	Country Fare	Doreen Fulleylove	80p
☐	Jewish Cookbook	Florence Greenberg	£1.50
☐	Know Your Onions	Kate Hastrop	95p
☐	Indian Cooking	Attia Hosain and Sita Pasricha	£1.50
☐	Home Preserving and Bottling	Gladys Mann	80p
☐	Home Baked Breads & Cakes	Mary Norwak	75p
☐	The Slim Gourmet	Lou Seibert Pappas	£1.50
☐	Easy Icing	Marguerite Patten	95p
☐	Wine Making at Home	Francis Pinnegar	£1.25
☐	Cooking for Christmas & Other Feasts	Shona Crawford Poole	£1.50
☐	Microwave Cookbook	Jill Spencer	£1.25
☐	Mixer and Blender Cookbook	Myra Street	80p
☐	The Diabetic Cookbook	Elisabeth Russell Taylor	£1.50
☐	The Hamlyn Pressure Cookbook	Jane Todd	85p
☐	Home Made Country Wines	Dorothy Wise	75p
☐	A Comprehensive Guide to Deep Freezing		65p

NON-FICTION

HUMOUR

☐ Don't Quote Me	Atyeo & Green	£1.00
☐ Ireland Strikes Back!	Seamus B. Gorrah	85p
☐ Pun Fun	Compiled by Paul Jennings	95p
☐ 1,001 Logical Laws	Compiled by John Peers	95p
☐ The Devil's Bedside Book	Leonard Rossiter	85p
☐ Colin Welland's Anthology of Northern Humour		£1.25

GAMES AND PASTIMES

☐ The Hamlyn Book of Wordways 1		75p

GARDENING/HOBBIES

☐ 'Jock' Davidson's House Plant Book		£1.50
☐ A Vegetable Plot for Two – or More	D. B. Clay Jones	£1.00
☐ Salads the Year Round	Joy Larkcom	£1.50
☐ Fred Loads' Gardening Tips of a Lifetime		£1.50
☐ Sunday Telegraph Patio Gardening		
(revised illustrated edition)	Robert Pearson	£3.95
☐ Greenhouse Gardening	Sue Phillips	£1.25

COOKERY

☐ A to Z of Health Foods	Carol Bowen	£1.50
☐ The Giant Sandwich Book	Carol Bowen	£1.25
☐ Vegetarian Cookbook	Dave Dutton	£1.50
☐ Country Fare	Doreen Fulleylove	80p
☐ Jewish Cookbook	Florence Greenberg	£1.50
☐ Know Your Onions	Kate Hastrop	95p
☐ Indian Cooking	Attia Hosain and Sita Pasricha	£1.50
☐ Home Preserving and Bottling	Gladys Mann	80p
☐ Home Baked Breads & Cakes	Mary Norwak	75p
☐ The Slim Gourmet	Lou Seibert Pappas	£1.50
☐ Easy Icing	Marguerite Patten	95p
☐ Wine Making at Home	Francis Pinnegar	£1.25
☐ Cooking for Christmas & Other Feasts	Shona Crawford Poole	£1.50
☐ Microwave Cookbook	Jill Spencer	£1.25
☐ Mixer and Blender Cookbook	Myra Street	80p
☐ The Diabetic Cookbook	Elisabeth Russell Taylor	£1.50
☐ The Hamlyn Pressure Cookbook	Jane Todd	85p
☐ Home Made Country Wines	Dorothy Wise	75p
☐ A Comprehensive Guide to Deep Freezing		65p

POCKET HEALTH GUIDES

☐ Migraine	Dr Finlay Campbell	65p
☐ Pre-menstrual Tension	June Clark	65p
☐ Back Pain	Dr Paul Dudley	65p
☐ Allergies	Robert Eagle	65p
☐ Asthma	Robert Eagle	85p
☐ Arthritis & Rheumatism	Dr Luke Fernandes	65p
☐ Cystitis	Diane Fernyhough	85p
☐ Circulation Problems	J. A. Gillespie	85p
☐ Depression and Anxiety	Dr Arthur Graham	85p
☐ Anaemia	Dr Alexander D. G. Gunn	85p
☐ Diabetes	Dr Alexander D. G. Gunn	85p
☐ Heart Trouble	Dr Simon Joseph	85p
☐ High Blood Pressure	Dr James Knapton	85p
☐ Peptic Ulcers	Drs Martin & Stiel	85p
☐ Hysterectomy	Wendy Savage	85p
☐ The Menopause	Studd & Thom	85p
☐ Skin Troubles	Deanna Wilson	65p
☐ Children's Illnesses	Dr Luke Zander	85p

GENERAL

☐ The Chinese Mafia	Fenton Bresler	£1.50
☐ Here Comes Everybody	Anthony Burgess	£1.75
☐ The Piracy Business	Barbara Conway	£1.50
☐ Basil Ede's Birds	Dougall & Ede	£4.95
☐ Strange Deaths	John Dunning	£1.50
☐ Truly Murderous	John Dunning	£1.50
☐ Ielfstan's Place	Richard Girling	£1.95

ZENITH

☐ The Way of a Transgressor	Negley Farson	£2.95
☐ A Child Possessed	R. C. Hutchinson	£2.50
☐ Days of Greatness	Walter Kempowski	£2.95
☐ The Beautiful Years	Henry Williamson	£2.50
☐ Dandelion Days	Henry Williamson	£2.50

HAMLYN PAPERBACKS

GENERAL FICTION

☐ The Patriarch	Chaim Bermant	£1.75
☐ The Free Fishers	John Buchan	£1.50
☐ Midwinter	John Buchan	£1.50
☐ A Prince of the Captivity	John Buchan	£1.50
☐ The Eve of Saint Venus	Anthony Burgess	£1.10
☐ Nothing like the Sun	Anthony Burgess	£1.50
☐ The Wanting Seed	Anthony Burgess	£1.50
☐ Mildred Pierce	James M. Cain	£1.50
☐ Past All Dishonour	James M. Cain	£1.25
☐ My Father's House	Kathleen Conlon	£1.50
☐ Pope Joan	Lawrence Durrell	£1.35
☐ The Country of Her Dreams	Janice Elliott	£1.35
☐ Secret Places	Janice Elliott	£1.35
☐ Letter to a Child Never Born	Oriana Fallaci	£1.00
☐ A Man	Oriana Fallaci	£1.95
☐ The Bride of Lowther Fell	Margaret Forster	£1.75
☐ Marital Rites	Margaret Forster	£1.50
☐ The Big Goodnight	Judy Gardiner	£1.25
☐ Who Was Sylvia?	Judy Gardiner	£1.50
☐ Duncton Wood	William Horwood	£1.95
☐ Styx	Christopher Hyde	£1.50
☐ Passing Through	Guida Jackson	£1.25
☐ A Bonfire	Pamela Hansford Johnson	£1.50
☐ The Good Husband	Pamela Hansford Johnson	£1.50
☐ The Good Listener	Pamela Hansford Johnson	£1.50
☐ The Honours Board	Pamela Hansford Johnson	£1.50
☐ The Unspeakable Skipton	Pamela Hansford Johnson	£1.50
☐ Kine	A. R. Lloyd	£1.50
☐ Dingley Falls	Michael Malone	£1.95
☐ Highland Fling	Nancy Mitford	£1.50
☐ Pigeon Pie	Nancy Mitford	£1.50
☐ The Red Raven	Lilli Palmer	£1.25
☐ Cocaine	Pitigrilli	£1.50
☐ An Inch of Fortune	Simon Raven	£1.25
☐ Celestial Navigation	Anne Tyler	£1.00
☐ The Clock Winder	Anne Tyler	£1.50
☐ If Morning Ever Comes	Anne Tyler	£1.50
☐ Morgan's Passing	Anne Tyler	£1.50
☐ Searching for Caleb	Anne Tyler	£1.00

CRIME/ADVENTURE/SUSPENSE

☐ The Blunderer	Patricia Highsmith	£1.50
☐ A Game for the Living	Patricia Highsmith	£1.50
☐ Those Who Walk Away	Patricia Highsmith	£1.50
☐ The Tremor of Forgery	Patricia Highsmith	£1.50
☐ The Two Faces of January	Patricia Highsmith	£1.50

FICTION

CRIME WHODUNNITS

☐ Some Die Eloquent	Catherine Aird	£1.25
☐ The Case of the Abominable Snowman	Nicholas Blake	£1.10
☐ The Widow's Cruise	Nicholas Blake	£1.25
☐ The Worm of Death	Nicholas Blake	95p
☐ Thou Shell of Death	Nicholas Blake	£1.25
☐ Green for Danger	Christiana Brand	£1.10
☐ Tour de Force	Christiana Brand	£1.10
☐ The Long Divorce	Edmund Crispin	£1.50
☐ A Leaven of Malice	Claire Curzon	£1.50
☐ King and Joker	Peter Dickinson	£1.25
☐ A Pride of Heroes	Peter Dickinson	£1.50
☐ The Four False Weapons	John Dickinson Carr	£1.25
☐ A Lonely Place to Die	Wessel Ebersohn	£1.10
☐ Gold from Gemini	Jonathan Gash	£1.10
☐ The Grail Tree	Jonathan Gash	£1.00
☐ The Judas Pair	Jonathan Gash	95p
☐ Spend Game	Jonathan Gash	£1.25
☐ Blood and Judgment	Michael Gilbert	£1.10
☐ Close Quarters	Michael Gilbert	£1.10
☐ Death of a Favourite Girl	Michael Gilbert	£1.50
☐ The Etruscan Net	Michael Gilbert	£1.25
☐ The Night of the Twelfth	Michael Gilbert	£1.25
☐ Hare Sitting Up	Michael Innes	£1.10
☐ Silence Observed	Michael Innes	£1.00
☐ There Came Both Mist and Snow	Michael Innes	95p
☐ The Weight of the Evidence	Michael Innes	£1.10
☐ The Tanglewood Murder	Lucille Kallen	£1.50
☐ The Howard Hughes Affair	Stuart Kaminsky	£1.10
☐ Go West, Inspector Ghote	H. R. F. Keating	£1.50
☐ Inspector Ghote Draws a Line	H. R. F. Keating	£1.10
☐ Inspector Ghote Plays a Joker	H. R. F. Keating	£1.25
☐ The Murder of the Maharajah	H. R. F. Keating	£1.25
☐ The Perfect Murder	H. R. F. Keating	£1.10
☐ Sweet and Deadly	Freny Olbrich	£1.25
☐ A Fine and Private Place	Ellery Queen	£1.00
☐ The French Powder Mystery	Ellery Queen	£1.25
☐ The Roman Hat Mystery	Ellery Queen	£1.50
☐ The Siamese Twin Mystery	Ellery Queen	95p
☐ The Spanish Cape Mystery	Ellery Queen	£1.10
☐ Murder for Treasure	David Williams	£1.50

NAME ....

ADDRESS ....

....

Write to Hamlyn Paperbacks Cash Sales, PO Box 11, Falmouth, Cornwall TR10 9EN.

Please indicate order and enclose remittance to the value of the cover price plus:

U.K.: Please allow 45p for the first book plus 20p for the second book and 14p for each additional book ordered, to a maximum charge of £1.63.

B.F.P.O. & EIRE: Please allow 45p for the first book plus 20p for the second book and 14p per copy for the next 7 books, thereafter 8p per book.

OVERSEAS: Please allow 75p for the first book and 21p per copy for each additional book.

Whilst every effort is made to keep prices low it is sometimes necessary to increase cover prices and also postage and packing rates at short notice. Hamlyn Paperbacks reserve the right to show new retail prices on covers which may differ from those previously advertised in the text or elsewhere.